THE SECRET BOOK OF SPY HUMOR

VOLUME THREE

Two Spies Walk Into A Bar

// //

ALSO BY THE AUTHOR

Stories from Langley: A Glimpse Inside the CIA

Briefing for the Boardroom and the Situation Room: A Brief Guidebook

The Counterintelligence Chronology:
Spying by and Against the United States from the 1700s Through 2014

The Secret Book of CIA Humor

The Secret Book of Intelligence Community Humor

Coaching Winning Model United Nations Teams

Food with Thought: The Wit and Wisdom of Chinese Fortune Cookies

The 50 Worst Terrorist Attacks

Terrorism Worldwide, 2017

Terrorism Worldwide, 2016

Terrorism 2013-2015: A Worldwide Chronology

Terrorism, 2008-2012: A Worldwide Chronology

Terrorism, 2005-2007: A Chronology

Terrorism, 2002-2004: A Chronology

Terrorism, 1996-2001: A Chronology

Terrorism, 1988-1991: A Chronology

International Terrorism in the 1980s: A Chronology of Events 1984-1987

International Terrorism in the 1980's: A Chronology of Events, 1980-1983

Transnational Terrorism: A Chronology of Events, 1968-1979

The Literature of Terrorism: A Selectively Annotated Bibliography

THE SECRET BOOK OF SPY HUMOR
//VOLUME THREE//

TWO SPIES WALK INTO A BAR . . .

EDWARD MICKOLUS

WW
WANDERING WOODS
PUBLISHERS

Two Spies Walk Into A Bar

By Edward F. Mickolus, PhD

First Edition May 2018

ISBN-13: 978-1-949173-01-7

Published in the United States by Wandering Woods Publishers

Book Design, Cover and Typesetting by
Cynthia J. Kwitchoff (CJKCREATIVE.COM)

WW
WANDERING
WOODS
PUBLISHERS

ABOUT THE AUTHOR

Edward F. Mickolus, PhD served a 33-year career with the Central Intelligence Agency in analytical, operational, management, and staff positions in four Directorates. His work at the CIA included analysis of international terrorism and African politics, covert action, HUMINT collection, counterintelligence, public affairs, and recruitment. He is a recipient of the CIA Career Intelligence and the Clandestine Service Medals.

Dr. Mickolus has written over 30 books, teaches courses on intelligence tradecraft, and is the President of Vinyard Software whose International Terrorism Data Center provides the best publicly-available data on terrorists and events around the world. He received his PhD in Political Science at Yale University.

A recovering standup comic, he often gives presentations on his collection of 1,000 fashion-challenged neckties and collects classic automobiles.

ACKNOWLEDGMENTS

Thanks go to Randy Tauss, Barbara Dean, Susan Simmons, Michael Douglas Smith, Steve Richter, David Cariens, Greg Kmiecik, David Chizum, Ben Cates, Clint Mesle, Jon Hittle, Christopher (sorry, we're protecting his last name. He knows who he is.), Kurt, Timmy W.-Y-, Emil Levine, Brian G., Becky S., Dan K., the Association of Former Intelligence Officers, the CIA Retirees Association, and a host of colleagues who chose to remain anonymous, some because they're still under cover, some because they don't want their colleagues knowing that they were responsible for these practical jokes and thereby engage in retribution (which will be chronicled in volume 3 of this series!). Thanks also to ace proofreader Tim Lightfield and the always brilliant Cindy Kwitchoff.

DISCLAIMER

All statements of fact, opinion, or analysis expressed are those of the author and do not reflect the official positions or views of the CIA, the Office of the Director of National Intelligence, any other Intelligence Community organization, or any other US Government agency. Nothing in the contents should be construed as asserting or implying US Government authentication of information or Agency or ODNI endorsement of the author's views. This material has been reviewed by the CIA and Office of the Director of National Intelligence to prevent the disclosure of classified information. This wasn't the toughest review for the PRB, which once had to review a tattoo—the author did not say when it would be shown—and a gravesite.

TABLE OF CONTENTS

INTRODUCTION

Thank you so much for picking up this third book in my espionage humor trilogy. If you bought it, many more thanks. If you obtained it from the library, please tell your friends to buy their own copy. Who wants to read a "pre-read" book?

When I began this series, people would comment snidely, "What? Spies have humor?" Or "If you told me a spy joke, you'd have to kill me, right?" Looks like the joke's on them, with three volumes of material and going strong.

It's been heartening to write this series and see the reactions of people to it. I've aimed at making the intimidating world of espionage perhaps a little more approachable for readers, and let them see that we're all normal people (well, ok, dashing, attractive, adventurous, bon vivant heroes and heroines who save the world three times before breakfast, but still just normal people) with well-developed senses of humor. And if the audiences gets a few laughs out of it as well, great.

If you're a member of the Intelligence Community, either American or foreign, and have an item you'd like to see in Volume 4, please send it to me at mail to: vinyardsoftware@hotmail.com.

OK, enough of an introduction; on to the guffaws.

SPY SONG

Written by an NSA officer, to the tune of Brad Paisley's *I'm Still a Guy*:

I'm Still a Spy
When you see a mole
You think tunnels
And I see Hanssen
Up on the wall.
When you see a park
You think picnics
And I see a dead drop
Up under that log.
When you see a priceless French painting
I see terrorist financing
You'd like to buy one to hang on the wall
And I'd like to set up a sting.
Well, this job makes a man do some things he ain't proud of
And in a weak moment I might
Give up secret codes
Or quote "Chuck" episodes
But remember, I'm still a spy.

And I'll put out a bag, cover your head in the car
Ride around town until you talk
Then turn right around, knock you to the ground
And leave you right there in shock
I can hear you now talkin' to your friends
'Cause I work for the NSA
From your weekend plans to your ideal man
I know just what you say.
But when I say a work trip means only a work trip
And you're mad 'cause you can't know why
Well, now what can I say at the end of the day
Remember, I'm still a spy.
You're probably thinking that you're going to turn me
In some ways, well, maybe you might
Dress me down, butter me up
Oh, but no matter what,
Remember, I'm still a spy.
These days there's dudes getting HUMINT,
IMINT, and SIGINT with maps
With deep-cover plans and transnational clans
It's tough to fill knowledge gaps.
With all of these men signing up for the Twitter
It's hip now to be publicized
But I don't highlight my work
Or say my boss is a jerk.
Remember, I'm still a spy.
I'm not on Facebook
So don't even look
Oh, thank God,
I'm still a spy.

ONE-LINERS

The tyranny of Twitter's 140-character limit has arrived among the spies. The advent of social media inside the Intelligence Community offered many would-be standup comedians a chance to test out their one-liners. A few of my favorites:

- Typical themes in operations refer to money, betray, and lust for power. And those are just the things you need to get office space.
- The fact that I target "Persons of Interest" does not make them interesting people.
- What if the world really did end last week like the Mayans said, and hell is actually just watching Congress try to negotiate the fiscal cliff?
- Putting "sent from my iPhone" at the bottom of my classified emails gets the best responses...
- If I trip and fall in a conference room, and everyone is under cover, do I make a sound?
- I think that any government that denies knowledge is probably speaking the truth.
- They say you can kill a man but you can't kill an idea. I say, "any man I want?"

- I said he was a highly reliable, well-placed source. I never said what he had access to or what he was reliable for.
- I wish the fire alarm system would stop giving out little random bleeps and make up its mind. The suspense is Killing Me!
- Anyone have any Good Idea Fairy repellant I can borrow?
- Why do you always run into someone you haven't seen for years on the days you look your worst?
- It's kinda difficult to teach analysts about the perils of cognitive biases when the training leaders are more biased than anyone.
- Idiot Juice is falling from the sky for the 7th straight Tuesday.
- If you don't know what you are talking about…don't talk.
- Some people couldn't collaborate their way out of a locked car.
- One day my now ex-wife told me, "I want a divorce." I looked her right in the eye and said, "I knew we had something in common."
- Did you know cannibals won't eat divorced women because they're bitter?
- Every time a new Sharepoint site is created, a kitten dies. Why are you trying to kill kittens?
- When asked what movie most realistically depicted intel work, I answered "Office Space".
- Notice to all persons who make calls: If the person you're calling doesn't answer by the 9th ring, they most likely won't answer at the 20th.
- "Did you forget your badge?" "No, I just felt like wearing a giant stupid blue T today." (*Ed's note:* Temporary badges have a large T on them.)

- I kill terrorists with Powerpoint, I mean, pinpoint accuracy.
- How do you give an Unsung Hero Award? Isn't that contradictory? Your Earth logic is not wanted here!
- Studies show that the collective IC brainpower lost remembering passwords could have caught bin Laden 9.4 months earlier.
- I celebrated the Queen's Diamond Jubilee by refusing to quarter soldiers in my home.
- It's not a stovepipe, it's a cylinder of excellence.
- Sharepoint is to collaboration as Taco Bell is to Mexican food.
- The cubicle is the human equivalent of the hamster wheel. You're running and yet the view isn't changing.
- 100% of divorces start in marriage.
- "An unexpected error has occurred." No! It's not unexpected because I get that error every time I try to use this!
- My dream job allows me to use my ADHD to flit around to whatever is shiny at the moment and still contribute to the mission.
- A neutron walks into a bar and asks the price of a drink. The bartender replies, "For you, no charge!"
- Sense and security policy are generally only nodding acquaintances.
- I found out this weekend that my niece has a tan line on her hand from where she holds her phone.
- Intelligence: It's a job description, not a requirement.
- Alright, now let's go get Zawahiri. I'll drive.
- You never know when you'll have to feed 20 people on short notice, and all you have on hand are a couple of capybaras.

- First World Problems: Being heartbroken after you accidentally press the wrong button on a vending machine and get a snack you don't want.
- Kudos to whoever implemented outsourcing our most sensitive ops debriefs to the *Washington Post*. Now I can work from home!
- Debating my dietician: She says I need more veggies. I say I need more meat from a variety of animals that eat a multiplicity of plants.
- We regret to inform you that, due to budget cuts, the Pentagon is being reduced to a Square.
- Frutile: a conversation that bears a great deal of pointless, inedible fruit.
- The Sense of Humor store called. Your refund will be processed shortly.
- You ought to join terrible people even though you are technically not a person.
- The horse is dead. Long live the horse.
- I heard unprotected Olympics can result in a bad case of heptathlon.
- My supervisor didn't think it was funny when he asked for a "head count" and I told him how many bathrooms are in the building.
- Anyone can quit smoking. It takes a *real* man to tempt cancer.
- A Contrarian takes the opposite side of an argument. A Futilitarian takes the pointless side.
- Is "most blocked user" a potential category? If so, then I can confirm you.
- I'm just here for the Iranian nuclear reactor playing AC/DC's "Thunderstruck" discussion.

- The first rule of trolling is never admit you're trolling.
- Loose tweets sink fleets.
- I prefer the term "apatheist". I don't know what is or isn't true, but I do know I don't care.
- I just got a Microsoft word error that told me to reinstall my floppy drive.
- The 90's called…they want their phone back.
- That's the cruelty of a Tuesday. You think it's not Monday and never suspect that it could be a second Monday in disguise.
- Why am I not in a time zone where it's Friday?
- "Ah, Grad Thesis…I thought I recognized your foul stench!"
- In the Middle Ages you would have been stoned to death for this kind of spreadsheet offense.
- Just how messed up of an African nation do you have to be, to be the client state of another African nation?
- Hey, I was just thinking about you! In a good way. Work Related!
- Hey, whatever floats your boat. Just know that I laugh at your boat.
- Al Qaeda has been posting Internet ads offering training for suicide bombers.
- What always worried me was that the Illuminati had the same jingle as in the GE lighting commercials.
- Grammar: the difference between knowing your s--- and knowing you're s---.

Overheard in the Office

Another version of the one-liner is what is supposedly Overheard in the Office, including:

- NSA: where security is our middle name. And like most middle names, it gets ignored.
- I don't understand you hunters. Why don't you just get your meat at the grocery store, where no animals have been harmed?
- "Ready for the monthly brief?" "Yeah, I've loved nap time since kindergarten."
- I'm all about work-life balance. I may have to wear pants for 9 hours a day, but they come off as soon as I get home.
- If I were you, I'd just purge email, take a hammer to your computer, light your desk on fire, and go home.
- "This used to be a door?" "It still is."
- You're gonna need to rewrite that because I can herd your cats, but I ain't got enough lipstick for your pigs.
- "If stress causes hair loss, why does The Hulk have more hair than I do?" "Because your job really sucks."
- Your analysis is uglier than your haircut!
- Dick Clark died. And we just can't ring in the New Year without Dick Clark. Well played, Mayans, well played.
- You know the real reason the space shuttle had to circle around DC—they have parking for only 60% of the shuttle fleet.
- I farted during my polygraph. I'm 99% sure she knew I lied when I said it wasn't me.
- Well, after THAT brief, we are most definitely on the @$$ end of the spear.
- "My Mac never gets viruses!" "That's because even hackers think Mac users are special ed kids."
- In regards to the women of Iceland: "The gene pool there benefits from the facts that the Vikings didn't kidnap no uggos."

- You are an accident report waiting for a date-time group.
- I think what we need to focus on here is putting the "fun" back into "dysfunctional".
- What does this document mean? So many acronyms. Does anyone here speak military?
- Jiddah is the shopping Mecca of the world!
- There's not much damage that I can do that we can't recover from.
- Presenter, speaking of classification level: "We always try to keep this as low class as possible."
- You've heard of the "cone of silence"? Well, I work in the "triangle of apathy".
- We need game ideas for the office picnic. Do you know any games that don't involve alcohol or the removal of clothing?
- He was trying to impress me, talking about his new assignment; he dropped so many flashy acronyms, I'm gonna have to sweep.
- So he told 'em, "I can't come to work today. I forgot my clearance."
- Breaking news. Charges against Osama bin Laden have been dropped.
- Why would they hand such a low-level tasker to him? Talk about bringing a hand grenade to an arm wrestling contest...
- He's really good at using a lot of words to say absolutely nothing. I hear that is a career path unto itself.
- "I think you should see the nurse." "Why, is she cute?"
- Gorilla warfare? What's that about, fighting over bananas?
- Guess muj have cell phones in heaven. It makes sense. They probably have Virgin Mobile.

- Saying "no" just sounds so negative, so let's just say "yes" and blow it off.
- You're a "Glass half empty" kinda person, eh? I'm a "hey, look, it's a glass…whatever" kind of person.
- I'd take the Human Capital Survey, but even I don't care about my own opinion.
- "You forgot your badge?" "I'm here and I'm wearing pants. What more do you want?
- I want to set him on fire and roast marshmallows in the flames so that my s'mores taste like his defeat.
- "He was wounded and eventually died." "It was the Civil War. Eventually they all died."
- This operation would be a lot easier if the enemy didn't suck at their jobs so much.
- Hey, do you ever get the feeling that the NSA guy in the next cube is listening to our conversations?
- How about Bill Gates for President? You think government works bad, now? Wait until it works like Windows!
- We have a scheduled power outage this weekend. I feel powerless to do anything about it.
- *fire alarm goes off* "I told you not to go on that site!"
- My job can be boiled down to this: I put lipstick on your pig. So just tell me the truth.
- They said, "yes, maybe." So in other words, "stand by to stand by".
- "I think he's still at lunch." Well, either that, or he's somewhere else." "Very profound!"
- Well, it's a war movie, so there's no violence except for the war violence.

- This gumbo is good, but it's the tracer round of the digestive world.
- You keep using that word. Are you sure you understand what it means?
- "I wish I was IT literate." "I just wish you were literate, period."
- I know you're smoking your underwear with some of the stuff that comes out of your mouth.
- Somewhere, somebody's having a beer. It's not me.
- "I can't eat your sushi, it has avocado. Ew." "Fine, I'll make you a Midol roll next time."
- "Has plenty of opinions" I'm gonna start putting that at the bottom of my signature block.
- I would be a nudist if it weren't for the lack of pockets.
- You know you're a screw up when your name ceases to be a noun and becomes a verb.
- "I married my wife because she used to be hot." "I bet you used to be hot, too."
- There's a theory about no question being a dumb question. You just blew that theory away.
- "What would you say drives the IC?" "Schadenfreude and caffeine." *heavy sigh* "Yes, like that. I feel driven now."
- We're expecting the dead drop to be loaded with blame, so come prepared.
- I've seen 2-year-olds with forks and light socket access make better personal choices than you.
- *horrified look* We deployed HIM!? What, were the Girl Scouts busy?
- "This would be more formal…er. Formaler?" "Formalererer?" "Sure."

- Doc told me I need to avoid booze and caffeine for my overactive bladder. Thanks. I'll just pee my pants instead.
- We are definitively snatching defeat from the jaws of victory on that one.
- I think there's a language barrier here. Your language is very confusing, even to me.
- You could hit me if I ran down the muzzle of your weapon.
- "Bullets are a great cure for nasal congestion." "Too permanently disfiguring."

// 🌐 //

50 Ways to Terminate Your Asset

Other sites conduct humor contests, including 50 Ways to Terminate Your Asset, to be modeled on Paul Simon's "50 Ways to Leave Your Lover":

- Set him in front of copper, Topper.
- A big boom by Bronze, Fonz.
- Deny him a visa, Lisa.
- Abduct him in Rome, Noam.
- Get him indicted at the Hague, Craig.
- Throw him under a bus, Gus.
- Take away his Wii, Leah.
- Fire ants and honey, Bunny.
- Stab him in the back, Jack.
- Shoot him in the head, Ned.

// 🌐 //

You Know You Work for CIA. . . .

Another site learned how You Know You Work for CIA:

- I've answered the phone numerous times, "Public Works, this is Jody" and also just "Hello, this is Jody" which sounds funny when you are answering your cell phone this way.
- Lying feels natural.
- You yell at the TV, while watching 24, "You can't do that with a cell phone in a SCIF!" or "My computer can't do that!"

- You show your badge to the toll booth operator.
- You try to use your badge to enter the bathroom.
- You go into a public rest room and wonder why the water in the sink is not coming on when you wave your hand under it, or you walk away and wonder why the water is still running.
- Your vehicle starts to head in the direction of work on a Saturday or Sunday and that was Not the direction you were planning.
- I had a nightmare once that involved Lotus Notes (*Ed's note:* the Agency e-mail program.)
- You find yourself trying to classify your home e-mails.
- You try to lock your computer.
- Saying "I SameTimed" somebody in a general conversation. (*Ed's note:* the Agency instant messaging system)
- You go through a turnstyle and are looking to enter your PIN…somewhere!
- I once tried using my badge to enter my home. After I got into the garage I placed my badge where a badge reader would have been if I was going into my office.
- I went in Giant after work one night and for some reason there was a security guard at the door. I automatically pulled out my badge. The guard's response, "Uh, ma'am, I don't need to see that!"
- When you refer to going to the 7-11 as going to the blind man store. (*Ed's note:* Agency snack bars are run by a blind entrepreneurs' firm.)
- When you look at movies and TV shows about the Agency and classify them as Comedy instead of Action/Adventure.
- Instead of telling someone I'll e-mail them, I said I'll Notes them in a few.
- Hitting F9 to validate e-mail addresses on your gmail account.

- I had a computer problem at home one day. I reached over to where my desk phone usually is and hit 2 on the speed dial to call our Help Desk.
- Always looking in my rear view mirror to see if anyone is following me…going to Safeway!
- Seeing someone in the store on the weekends and realizing you can't say hello to them because you have no idea what their name really is and they do not know your name.
- When your manager invents an acronym to describe his lunch.
- You go back to school after the summer's over, and everyone starts telling everyone the details of their summer jobs/internships while you stand awkwardly off to the side, not saying anything.
- You see someone in a public place and you are about to say hello, but then realize you have no idea whether you "know" them in public.
- When a news article abbreviates tropical storm as TS and you wonder why a storm is classified.
- You laugh while watching a spy movie/show because their computers work.
- You try to badge out of the bathroom.
- I used my badge against the elevator light waiting for the door to open.
- You go to throw away trash at home and look for a burn bag.
- You no longer want to watch CNN "news" since you see/hear/read too much news at work.
- You are a bottomless well of information about places Americans aren't legally allowed to visit.
- When your spouse knows when it is time to change the subject of the conversation before you try to.
- You're getting paid extra just for appearing to be boring.

Social media can also lead to arguments about a host of issues, including proper grammar. Herewith, a discussion I was in:

Poster 1: ♋♐♎♎♋♐♏⍓♏⧫♐⬥⬥⍓🙵♎♒⌧⬥♒♎♐⬥♏◆
And that's the last I'm going to say on this.

Poster 2: I believe ♋♐♎♎♋♐ is normally spelled with a trailing ♏⬥ when used in a declarative sentence…

Poster 1: That is true EXCEPT when the sentence ends in a nominative absolute, as it does here.

//🌐//

Totalitarian Valentine's Day

The writers of one-liners can also be a romantic bunch, as evidenced by the Have a Very Totalitarian Valentine's Day Card posters:

- (photo of Leon Trotsky) Thinks you're hotsky.
- (photo of Hitler) Be Mein.
- (photo of Stalin) Quit Stalin. Be my Valentine.
- (photo of Fidel Castro) Don't embargo my love.
- (photo of Kim Jong Il) You're the Kim Jong Illest.
- (photo of Idi Amin) Amin love with you.
- (photo of Mao) You are the most honorable chairman of my heart.
- (Photo of Karl Marx) Roses are red. So is the state. Let us be comrades, because you are great.
- Vladimir Lenin: Be my Valenintine.
- Khrushchev: I will bury you…with love.
- Vladimir Putin: Quit Putin me off. Be mine.
- Hirohiti thinks you're neat-o.
- Mao thinks you're wow!

- I want to Lenin for a kiss…
- Generalissimo Francisco Franco: I'm still dead…to anybody but you.
- Che Guevara doesn't want to shara you.
- Putin will win your heart, like he (fairly) wins elections.
- Palpatine is keen on you.
- Dr. No wants you to say "yes".
- Slobadon't you wanna be my Valentine?
- Uganda ask me out?
- Kenya be my Valentine?
- I can't TU-95 BEAR the thought of not being with you.
- Khmer and be my Valentine
- (photo of Kim Jong Un) You are the Unly one for me.

COVER AND COVER SHEETS

In the 1970s the facility where I worked was a CIA Black Site. When you reported in there, you signed YET ANOTHER long secrecy agreement, promising NEVER to disclose that the facility was CIA, much less what kind of work went on there. Insofar as the public at large, it was a Black Site.

But there are formal smarts and there are street smarts. Every vagrant, bum, rummy, crack-head, thief, pimp and ne'er-do-well in that crummy old neighborhood knew EXACTLY what agency occupied the building. They smell cops a mile away. One day, there was a film crew from one of the major networks camped out on the sidewalk beyond our fence line with a perky little investigative reporter trying to file an exclusive report on the tenants of our facility.

As she walked along the sidewalk just outside the hurricane fence—and with Agency security officers nervously monitoring her—she started to ask passers-by if they lived in the neighborhood, and if they knew who was occupying the building. Finally she happened across a gray haired old black dude whose clothes were dirty and unkempt. He was sitting on the sidewalk with his back leaning up against the fence, nodding off from a poor night's sleep and a hangover and with a filthy old raincoat wrapped around him. Miss "Perky" spied him and she bounded over, stuck a microphone in this guy's face and asked him if he knew what was going on in the building on the other side of the fence. The old dude stared her straight in the eye, and with a solemn countenance on his grizzled face, he raised a forefinger up in front of his lips; in an alcoholic stupor he slurred the following reply, "Shhhhhhh! izza big secret! Jerking a thumb back toward the direction of our facility, he whispered, "Don't tell ANYONE... CIA!" If only the Russians had spent more time recruiting tramps in the area, it might have changed the whole Star Wars "Trust but Verify" deal.... We might have lost the Cold War.

// 🌐 //

For fire drills at the facility, the Office of Security reportedly had a liaison with the DC Fire Department, and during a fire drill, the fire fighters were supposed to act low key and never say the magic letters "CIA". Black Site and all, you know.

One day during a fire drill a replacement Captain from the DC Fire Department apparently never got the word. As we filed out into the large parking lot on that spring day, we were greeted by the voice of the fire Captain, standing on the sidewalk with a powered megaphone, just like Mayberry's Barney Fife: "ALRIGHT! I WANT ALL OF YOU CIA PEOPLE TO MOVE BRISKLY AWAY FROM THE BUILDING! QUICKLY NOW! HURRY UP CIA! HURRY UP CIA!"

Plainclothes Office of Security guys were tripping over each other to run at that guy to shut him up and wrestle that megaphone away from him. All of us were falling down laughing in the parking lot. If the Russians penetrated the DC Fire Department, it could have changed the whole strategic picture!

// 🌐 //

Hollywood revels in using cover sheets—a single sheet of paper put on top of a classified file to hide its contents from prying eyes—as props. TOP SECRET and SECRET, with supposedly appropriately colored red or blue borders, are particular favorites. Intelligence Community wags enjoy spoofing these daily warnings about the seriousness of the information contained within. Among them is one on DOOMINT, which became popular during the rise of "low probability-high impact" analysis of potential catastrophes:

DOOM!

This is a Cover Sheet for Apocalyptic Data

All individuals handling this information are required to protect it from any disclosure whatsoever in the interest of maintaining a false sense of hope.

Handling, storage, reproduction, or other association with the attached document is discouraged to avoid the possible recognition of how totally screwed we really are as a civilization.

(This cover sheet is disastrous.)

DOOM!

NSN Wezallgonnadie!

STANDARD FORM 666-Y2525
Prescribed by Gen Chaos

FUTILE

This is a Cover Sheet for Useless Information

All individuals handling this information are required to disregard it as rapidly as possible in the interest of saving time and effort.

Handling, storage, reproduction, and distribution of the attached document is discouraged to the maximum extent possible in order to prevent any more work being wasted on this project which will never amount to anything anyway.

(This cover sheet is a waste of paper.)

FUTILE

NSN 1000-or more-
wasted man-hours

STANDARD FORM Trash-me-Now
Prescribed by Maj Waste O Time

PATHETIC

This is a Cover Sheet for Pitiable Information

All individuals handling this information are required to maintain a straight race while stressing its importance to the future of the operation. At no time should common sense or critical thinking be applied to this information, as the resulting reaction could devastate the originating official's ego.

Handling, storage, reproduction, and distribution of the attached document is discouraged to the maximum extent possible to postpone the inevitable revelation that our organization is crippled by such petty stuff.

(This cover sheet is weaker than a quadriplegic poodle.)

PATHETIC

STANDARD FORM C-17
NSN Kenny G
Prescribed by CMSgt Desert Helpers

LUDICROUS

This is a Cover Sheet for Preposterous Information

All individuals handling this information are required to disregard all logic and common sense. Failure to do so may result in the collapse of reality as we know it.

Handling, storage, reproduction, and distribution of the attached document is irrelevant to all individuals concerned with it are already so confused that life, the universe, and everything have all become meaningless.

(If you can read this, you don't need glasses.)

LUDICROUS

STANDARD FORM 42
Prescribed by Maj Disaster

STUPID

This is a Cover Sheet for Asinine Information

All individuals handling this information are required to protect it from any disclosure whatsoever in the interest of our professional credibility.

Handling, storage, reproduction, or other association with the attached document is discouraged to avoid the possible assignment of total, partial, or remote responsibility for its contents.

(This cover sheet is demented.)

STUPID

STANDARD FORM Ump-D-Ump
NSN 17-10-24-HUT Prescribed by I.M.N. Idiot

BS

This is a Cover Sheet for BS Information

All individuals handling this information are required to wash their hands before serving food products or shaking hands with any other individuals not authorized to handle or disseminate BS.

Handling, storage, reproduction of the attached document without the proper level of authorization may result in the labeling as a BS'r.

(This cover sheet stinks.)

BS

NSN Oh-BS-Gimme-a-Break

CONFUSING

This is a Cover Sheet for Ambiguous Information

All individuals handling this information are required to disregard all logic and common sense. Failure to do so may result in severe migraines or an attack of conscience.

Handling, storage, reproduction, and distribution of the attached document is discouraged to the maximum extent possible in order to keep the contradicting, menial, and convoluted nature of this project hush-hush.

(This cover sheet is as clear as mud.)

CONFUSING

NSN Huh?

STANDARD FORM W.T.F.O.
Prescribed by We Todd Did

A GRATUITOUS BLONDE SPY JOKE, TOLD TO ME BY A WOMAN

Three female spies—a brunette, a redhead, and a blonde—had been captured and were awaiting execution. The evil enemy dictator ordered their execution: death by firing squad.

As they were all led from their cells into the courtyard, it looked like certain death. But the redhead had a plan! She whispered to the others, "I have an idea, just follow my lead."

The redhead was put up against the wall.

"Do you have any last words?" the evil dictator asked.

"No," she replied.

"Very well," said the dictator as he turned to his soldiers. "Ready – Aim –" "TORNADO!" yelled the redhead, pointing behind the troops. The gunmen all turned around, and she escaped!

The brunette and the blonde saw this and got the idea. Next it was the brunette's turn. The dictator marched her up to the wall in front of his soldiers.

"Do you have any last words?" he asked.

"No," she replied.

"Very well," said the dictator as he turned to his soldiers. "Ready – Aim –" "TIDAL WAVE!" yelled the brunette, pointing behind the troops. The gunmen all turned around, and she escaped, too!

The dictator was becoming frustrated, but now it was the blonde's turn. He marched her to the wall in front of his troops.

"Do you have any last words?" he asked, suspiciously.

"No," she replied.

"Very well," said the dictator as he turned to his soldiers. "Ready – Aim –" "FIRE!" yelled the blonde.

SPY GAMES

Although Robert Redford and Brad Pitt popularized the term, they didn't invent spy games. Here are a few played by denizens of CIA Headquarters:

Hello

The coin of the realm at CIA, particularly in the Directorate of Operations (now the National Clandestine Service), is the extent of one's network. In a real sense, when recruiting spies to steal secrets, it really is a matter of whom you know, rather than what you know. You care more about what they know. To keep one's networking skills sharp for overseas work, operations officers also try to know as many people as they can at Headquarters. One way to test one's network against one's colleagues is to walk in tandem down the hallway from your office to the cafeteria. You get a point for each person who says "hello" to you. No fair salting the score with saying "hello" first.

Bingo

Large organizations around the world have their own specialized language/patois/bafflegab to separate the cognoscenti from the wannabes. This slanguage is all the more helpful among spies, where you really are trying to cloak your meaning from those not "read in" to a program. But sometimes spies are treated to the specialized terminology of management consultants, who bring the managerial fad of the day—TQM, Six Sigma Blackbelt, Zero-Based Budgeting, you name it—to forced-attendance meetings. To break up the monotony, Agency officers hand out bingo cards with several of these specialized terms sprinkled onto the squares. You get to mark the box whenever the consultant uses the term in the Powerpointed presentation. Winner is the first to hit Bingo. One particularly popular version offered the following words sprayed in the 5x5 classic Bingo array, with the center square free:

Pointy end of the spear	Horizontally integrated	Bleeding Edge	Synergy	Impact (used as a verb)
Full service	Drinking the Kool-Aid	Touch base	Value-added	Spun up
Out of pocket	Tiger team	BINGO	Core Competency	Warfighter
Take (this) offline	Corporate values	Thinking outside the box	Buy-in	Single point of failure
Leverage	Enterprise	Exceed Expectations	Best practice(s)	Lean(ing) forward

Other versions include the following words, which have become popular within the Community:

Inside baseball	Kabuki dance	Broad brush	Séance reading	Drudge Report it
5 Year Plan it	Vet (as a verb)	Rice bowl	Drink the Kool aid	When it's all said and done
At the end of the day	Less to this than meets the eye	BINGO	In the know	Par for the course
Soda-strawing	Roundtable (as a verb)	Q-and-A (as a verb)	Dialogue (as a verb)	Self-licking ice cream cone
Smoke and mirrors	Soup to nuts	Level the playing field	Stovepiping	Chairborne Rangers

A related observation on this issue: If you're baffled by mangled verbiage, just remember that the best defense is a good offense. Just make up your own plausible-sounding nonsense phrases and slide them into conversations with the worst offenders. Walk up to the "inside baseball" person and let fly with something like "Bob's been tweaking the tiller because someone stoked his pony, so we all just greased the peanut. Funny, huh?" You've won if they repeat any of your made-up phrases to others.

// 🌐 //

Fob-ulous Poker

On occasion, security officers attempt to improve computer security ("safe hex") by instituting fobs—small random-number generators—that are synched to one's desktop computer. Computer users must type in not only their password, but also the random number, which recycles after a specified number of seconds. The random numbers can also be used to develop poker hands. You have to be quick to show your winning hand, however—those fobs change numbers often!

Haikus

In honor of the 50th anniversary of the Cuban Missile Crisis, members of the Intelligence Community hosted a Haiku contest. Among the entries:

The world is tricky
Nuclear Armageddon
So, duck and cover.

Russians weren't crazy,
Nine to one in our favor,
Crisis overhyped.

Premier Khrushchev
POTUS says get the heck out
Bye bye Soviets.

Oh Beisbolista
Washington pitcher failure
Causes end of world.

Crisis averted!
Missiles removed from Cuba
Che would have fired them.

Missiles to the south;
Why do Boomers seem to think
China will repeat?

Nitze bests Kennan
Our missiles are in Turkey
Theirs are in Cuba.

The children never asked why
There were "Earthquake drills"
In Portland, Oregon.

An island of dread
Missiles are ready to launch
The world holds its breath.

DC Bobby Jack
Cuba Fidel Nikita
Poker with high stakes.

F-8 Crusader
Missiles in Cuba it saw
Returned with shrapnel.

Launch the torpedo?
Vasili Arkhipov says,
No nuclear war.

Cuban communists
Want to enter the arms race
Er um uh no way.

Khrushchev's brilliant plan:
Brinkmanship! What could go wrong?
Epic trolling fail.

The world by a thread
We crawl under our desks and
Ponder the cockroach.

This close to midnight
But we all expect a view
As bright as the sun.

Fall foliage shines for
Thirteen days in October
Not like it could have.

For once Kennedy
Enforced the Monroe Doctrine
Without Marilyn.

Since Khrushchev's defunct
Can Turkey get the nukes back
When Castro is gone?

The Cuban crisis
As contests go this one's gone
Like Russian missiles.

Name That Month

Given the popularity of Rocktober among the younger demographic, a contest was held for the in-crowd nickname for the following month. Entries included:

- Schmovember
- Dynamovember
- Go-go-govemberpower
- Turkeymonth
- @Month11
- Anti-May
- AlmostChristmasavember

- Godzillavember
- Americavember
- Howie

//🌐//

Art contests were fair game for the annual employee art contest at NSA. In 1968, the new NSA operations building opened, although construction was not complete in the connecting passageway. A Navy Field Operational Intelligence Office analyst installed a frame around an open electrical switch box containing many colored wires. He then transferred a second prize ribbon from a winning picture to the frame, where it remained until the end of the exhibit.

//🌐//

Corny Jokes

Among the scores of jokes submitted by the denizens of one particularly popular discussion site:

Q: How many NRA spokespersons does it take to change a lightbulb?
A: More guns.

Knock knock
Who's there?
Who.
Who who?
What are you, an owl?

I hate explaining puns to kleptomaniacs. They always take everything literally.

I heard puns about Pyromaniacs are hot right now.

I'm reading a book on anti-gravity. I just can't put it down.
Is it an uplifting book?

Did you hear about the two guys who stole a calendar? They both got six months.
I heard that 6 was afraid of 7 because 7 8 9.

I thought it was because 7 was a registered 6 offender.

Didja hear the joke about 288? It's two (too) gross.

When I get married I am going to ask Chick-fil-A to cater just to see if they would.

I prefer sax to violins.

I didn't get into the School of Hard Knocks, so I went to the less prestigious Academy of Light Slaps.

Stalking: it's a romantic walk between two people in the park…however, only one person knows this.

I think people only walk past my office when I am stretching, yawning, spilling coffee on myself, or otherwise appearing odd.

The traffic gods smiled on me today. Apparently you need to sacrifice a squirrel to get their attention.

A magician was on his way home and then he turned into a driveway.

A couple lived near the ocean and used to walk the beach a lot. One summer they noticed a girl who was at the beach pretty much every day. She wasn't unusual, nor was the travel bag she carried, except for one thing: she would approach people who were sitting on the beach, glance around furtively, then speak to them.

Generally, the people would respond negatively and she would wander off, but occasionally someone would nod and there would be a quick exchange of money for something she carried in her bag. The couple assumed she was selling drugs and debated calling the cops, but since they didn't know for sure, they just continued to watch her.

After two weeks, the wife asked, "Honey, have you ever noticed that she only goes up to people with boom boxes and other electronic devices?" He said he hadn't.

Then she said, "Tomorrow I want you to get a towel and our big radio and go lie on the beach. Then we can find out what she's really doing."

The plan went off without a hitch, and the wife was almost hopping up and down with anticipation when she saw the girl talk to her husband and then leave. The man walked up the beach and met his wife at the road. "Well, is she selling drugs?" she asked excitedly.

"No, she's not," he said, enjoying this probably more than he should have.

"Well, what is it, then?" his wife fairly shrieked.

The man grinned and said, "She's a battery salesperson."

"Batteries?" cried the wife.

"Yes," he said. "She sells C-cells by the seashore."

Did you ever notice that in all the pictures and documentaries about penguins, you never see a dead penguin? There is a reason for that. Most people know that penguins are very family-oriented animals; they mate for life and bring up offspring together. They also share in their food gathering and in braving the hardships of Arctic storms. When a penguin dies, the community comes together to the body of the deceased and uniformly starts pecking the ice around the dead penguin. Eventually the body of the penguin falls into the frozen sea. The penguins then gather around the hole in the ice and chant "freeze a jolly good fellow, freeze a jolly good fellow."

How do you catch a polar bear? You cut a big hole in the ice and sprinkle peas around the hole. Then, when the bear comes up to take a pea, you kick him in the ice hole.

You strangled that person with a rope? You're going to jail.
You bludgeoned that person with a bat? You're going to jail.
You stabbed that person with a knife? You're going to jail.
You ran that person over with a car? You're going to jail.

You cyber-bullied that person to the point of committing suicide?
You're going to jail.
You beat that person to death with your bare hands?
You're going to jail.
You shot that person with a gun? Get Rid of All The Guns!

There's something about pressing F5 that's just so…refreshing!

One man's fish is another man's poisson.

A vulture walks onto an airplane carrying 3 dead rabbits. The flight attendant stops him and says, "I'm sorry, sir, you are only allowed 2 carrion."

// 🌐 //

The Game That Circled the Globe

Back in the late 1970s, a base, sporting a lot of big white radome-covered satellite-tracking dishes, was having a slow day somewhere in the Southern and Eastern Hemispheres. Call it the Space Place. Come to find out, it also was a slow day back at an operations center in the Washington, D.C., area. Call it the Watch Bunch.

We guys on the other side of the world were testing a new communications system, which allowed for some flexibility in the signals we were sending back to D.C. It so happened that a big Washington Redskins game had been blacked out in the local area because the stadium seats hadn't been sold out. And the bored Watch Bunch were chomping at the bit to get some real-time football intelligence. Could the Space Place give assistance?

Oh, yezzz! Of course we could. There at the Space Place, we all knew that, in addition to thousands of foreign signals out there in cyberspace, our trusty satellite could receive and retransmit a clear signal from an AFRTS (Armed Forces Radio and Television Service) station in Germany. So we dialed it up, found the play-by-play narrative, and sent this latest live "test signal" across the Pacific and all of North America to our football-deprived colleagues back in the Redskin Zone.

As it bounced up and down via four geosynchronous satellites and five ground stations completely circling the globe, the signal had traveled over 178,000 miles, almost the distance to the moon. If it had come directly from the game to the Watch Bunch, the broadcast would have traveled less than 30 miles. But science and technology proved up to the challenge. The fans at the Watch Bunch heard the round-the-world game loud and clear.

MORE FUNNY THINGS ON THE WAY TO THE OPS MEETING

I was driving my asset back from a successful car meeting. It had gone well, but we started to become concerned when a local monsoon kicked up. At least it made it tough for surveillance to follow us safely. I didn't see them anywhere near us, so I proceeded to our dropoff point. As I looked around to make sure that the coast was clear, I heard the passenger door open. I didn't see the asset get out, and didn't see him anywhere near the car, so I closed the door and drove off. At the next meeting, he was furious with me. "How could you leave me like that?! How is this a way to treat me?!" he demanded to know. I said "Calm down. I don't know what you're talking about. What do you mean?" He said, "When I stepped out of the car, I discovered that you'd parked us right next to a manhole, and I fell in. I tried to grab the side of the car, but you drove off!"

// 🌐 //

Living documents—much like wikis, which are constantly edited/updated/defaced—are very popular within the IC. Among them is the list of Things SpyGuy is No Longer Allowed to Do on Covert Ops:

- Plan B is not automatically twice as much explosives as Plan A.
- An aerosol burst of Nair is not Plan A.
- Collateral Damage Man is not an appropriate operational callsign.
- Any officer who has a sensitivity training center named after him is not an appropriate mentor.
- I am not to kill off all the liaison service, even if they are terminally stupid.
- Synchronized panicking is not a proper ops plan.
- No longer allowed to set Nazi propaganda music to a snappy disco beat.
- Even if it's "True to James Bond," female officers' callsigns cannot be double entendres.
- No longer allowed to use the Blackhawk for booty calls.
- In the middle of a black op I cannot ask a guard to validate parking.
- My voucher for the purchase of 10,000 marbles will always be rejected, even if I say please.
- So will my voucher for any animal in groups of 100 or more.
- A picture of my ex-wife is not an acceptable backup weapon.
- My chain of command is not going to replace my performance evaluation process with a straight experience point award system.
- If the gun can't fit through the x-ray machine, it doesn't go on the plane.
- I cannot insert the words "Kill Phil…sorry, Phil" into any list of instructions.
- Not allowed to download AOL 6.0 onto the Chinese government's mainframe.
- Giving a four-year-old a sugar rush and pointing him at my surveillant is not proper demeanor.
- I should restrict the amount of taxpayers' money I give to pole dancers as tips.

- Claiming pole dancer tips as "humanitarian aid" is not a way around that.
- Driving through the streets broadcasting Shatner's spoken word album is in fact a violation of the Geneva Convention.
- If a black op requires me to impersonate an employee, I cannot bill the target for overtime.
- "Superfluous" is not an acceptable codename for "liaison".
- A covert action plan consisting entirely of "transform and roll out!" will be rejected.
- At the end of an entry op, I cannot crank call SWAT on the target's phone.
- I have been assured with total certainty that Ralph is not a usual Korean name.
- I am not from Margaritaville, and do not get alias docs from there.
- When installing a beacon on the target's vehicle, I can't install the Clapper as a built-in feature.
- No US intelligence agency has a 20,000-pigeon flock that's controllable by remote, even if I read it on the Internet.
- And even if we did, I can't have it.
- I cannot put anything featuring Calvin on my government vehicle.
- I am forbidden from convincing the tech ops officer to merge the best features of automatic weapons and manual transmissions.
- After a successful entry op, I will not leave paint bombs under all the boardroom's seat cushions.
- If the local service wakes to find a car upside down in a fountain, I'd better not be the prime, usual, or only suspect.
- All participants will use the bathroom before the entry op, not during.
- When in said bathroom, after entry op, but not for purposes of intended use, will not engage in close proximity martial arts, but will call legitimate "time out" with co-combatant,

and move engagement to living room where larger environment and more suitable breakable material exists.

- There is no conceivable reason for anyone in my career service to request 10 gallons of industrial lubricant.
- We will not implement any ops plan that includes the underlined words "and hope they miss a lot".
- I will not eat beans before entry op requiring close formation of which I am the leader.
- I will not take souvenirs from lingerie drawer of house we are covertly bugging.
- I will not make mix-tapes of phone sex from covertly bugged suspects and post them on-line.
- I will not append every mission statement from team lead with the words "in bed".
- I will not ever ever ever again covertly bug manager's house and replay manager farting/singing/blowing nose in shower.
- I will not blatantly misuse work terms like "covert entry" and "friendly fire" for close personal relationships lasting only one night.

OVERHEAD RECONNAISSANCE RULES

The Laws of Aviation

Though I Fly Through the Valley of Death ... I Shall Fear No Evil. For I am at 80,000 Feet and Climbing! *(Sign over the entrance to the old SR-71 operating base at Kadena, Japan.)*

✈

You've never been lost until you've been lost at Mach 3 *(Paul F. Crickmore -test pilot)*

✈

The only time you have too much fuel is when you're on fire.

✈

Blue water Navy truism: There are more planes in the ocean than submarines in the sky. *(From an old carrier sailor)*

✈

If the wings are traveling faster than the fuselage, it's probably a helicopter and therefore, unsafe.

✈

When one engine fails on a twin-engine airplane you always have enough power left to get you to the scene of the crash.

✈

Without ammunition, the USAF would be just another expensive flying club.

✈

What is the similarity between air traffic controllers and pilots? If a pilot screws up, the pilot dies; If ATC screws up ... the pilot dies.

✈

Never trade luck for skill.

✈

The three most common expressions (or famous last words) in aviation are: "Why is it doing that?", "Where are we?" and "Oh S--t!!!!"

✈

Weather forecasts are horoscopes with numbers.

✈

Progress in airline flying: Now a flight attendant can get a pilot pregnant.

✈

Airspeed, altitude and brains. Two are always needed to successfully complete the flight.

✈

A smooth landing is mostly luck; two in a row is all luck; three in a row is prevarication.

✈

I remember when sex was safe and flying was dangerous.

✈

Mankind has a perfect record in aviation; we never left anyone up there!

✈

Flashlights are tubular metal containers kept in a flight bag for the purpose of storing dead batteries!

✈

Flying the airplane is more important than radioing your plight to a person on the ground incapable of understanding or doing anything about it.

✈

When a flight is proceeding incredibly well, something was forgotten.

Just remember, if you crash because of weather, your funeral will be held on a sunny day.

✈

Advice given to RAF pilots during WWII: When a prang (crash) seems inevitable, endeavor to strike the softest, cheapest object in the vicinity as slowly and gently as possible.

✈

The Piper Cub is the safest airplane in the world; ...it can just barely kill you. *(Attributed to Max Stanley, Northrop test pilot)*

✈

The Altitude above you, the runway behind you, and the fuel not in the plane are totally worthless! *(Sonny Kellum, Flight Instructor)*

✈

A pilot's job is very simple.... there are 3 lights on an aircraft, red on left wing tip, green on right wing tip, white on the tail...Your job, as a pilot is to keep the plane between these 3 lights! *(Sonny Kellum, Flight Instructor)*

✈

A pilot who doesn't have any fear probably isn't flying his plane to its maximum. *(Jon McBride, astronaut)*

✈

If you're faced with a forced landing, fly the thing as far into the crash as possible. *(Bob Hoover - renowned aerobatic and test pilot)*

✈

Never fly in the same cockpit with someone braver than you!

✈

There is no reason to fly through a thunderstorm in peacetime. *(Sign over squadron OPS desk at Davis-Monthan AFB, AZ, 1970.)*

✈

The three best things in life are a good landing, a good orgasm, and a good bowel movement. The night carrier landing is one of the few opportunities in life where you get to experience all three at the same time. *(Author unknown, but surely someone who's been there)*

✈

If something hasn't broken on your helicopter, it's about to!

✈

Try to stay in the middle of the air. Do not go near the edges of it. The edges of the air can be recognized by the appearance of ground, buildings, sea, trees and interstellar space. It is much more difficult to fly there.

The two most abundant things in the universe are Hydrogen and stupidity and I don't know which is the most.

A Vietnam War helicopter pilot added these rules of life:

1. Once you are in the fight, it is way too late to wonder if this is a good idea.

2. It is a fact that helicopter tail rotors are instinctively drawn toward trees, stumps, rocks, etc. While it may be possible to ward off this natural event some of the time, it cannot, despite the best efforts of the crew, always be prevented. It's just what they do.

3. NEVER get into a fight without more ammunition than the other guy.

4. The engine RPM and the rotor RPM must BOTH be kept in the GREEN. Failure to heed this commandment can affect the morale of the crew.

5. Cover your buddy, so he can be around to cover for you.

6. Decisions made by someone above you in the chain-of-command will seldom be in your best interest.

7. The terms Protective Armor and Helicopter are mutually exclusive.

8. Sometimes, being good and lucky is still is not enough.

9. "Chicken Plates" are not something you order in a restaurant

10. If everything is as clear as a bell, and everything is going exactly as planned, you're about to be surprised.

11. Loud, sudden noises in a helicopter WILL get your undivided attention.

12. The BSR (Bang Stare Red) Theory states that the louder the sudden bang in the helicopter, the quicker your eyes will be drawn to the gauges. The longer you stare at the gauges the less time it takes them to move from green to red.

13. No matter what you do, the bullet with your name on it will get you. So, too, can the ones addressed "To Whom It May Concern".

14. If the rear echelon troops are really happy, the front line troops probably do not have what they need.

15. If you are wearing body armor, they will probably miss that part.

16. Happiness is a belt-fed weapon.

17. Having all your body parts intact and functioning at the end of the day beats the alternative.

18. If you are allergic to lead, it is best to avoid a war zone.

19. It is a bad thing to run out of airspeed, altitude, and ideas all at the same time.

20. Hot garrison chow is better than hot C-rations which, in turn, are better than cold C-rations which, in turn, are better than no food at all. All of these, however, are preferable to cold rice balls, even if they do have the little pieces of fish in them.

21. Everybody's a hero...On the ground...In the club...After the fourth drink.

22. A free fire zone has nothing to do with economics.

23. The further you fly into the mountains, the louder the strange engine noises become.

24. Medals are OK, but having your body and all your friends in one piece at the end of the day is better.

25. Being shot hurts.

26. "Pucker Factor" is the formal name of the equation that states the more hairy the situation is, the more of the seat cushion will be sucked up your ass. It can be expressed in its mathematical formula of S (suction) + H (height above ground) + I (interest in staying alive) + T (# of tracers coming your way).

27. Thus the term '@#$!' can also be used to denote a situation where high Pucker Factor is being encountered.

28. Thousands of Vietnam Veterans earned medals for bravery every day. A few were even awarded.

29. Running out of pedal, fore or aft cyclic, or collective are all bad ideas. Any combination of these can be deadly.

30. There is only one rule in war: When you win, you get to make up the rules.

31. C-4 can make a dull day fun.

32. There is no such thing as a fair fight - only ones where you win or lose.

33. If you win the battle you are entitled to the spoils. If you lose you don't care.

34. Nobody cares what you did yesterday or what you are going to do tomorrow. What is important is what you are doing - NOW - to solve our problem.

35. Always make sure someone has a P-38. Uh, that's a can opener for those of you who aren't military.

36. Prayer may not help...but it can't hurt.

37. Flying is better than walking. Walking is better than running. Running is better than crawling. All of these, however, are better than extraction by Medevac, even if it is technically a form of flying.

38. If everyone does not come home, none of the rest of us can ever fully come home, either.

39. Do not fear the enemy, for your enemy can only take your life. It is far better that you fear the media, for they will steal your HONOR.

40. A grunt is the true reason for the existence of the helicopter. Every helicopter flying in Vietnam had one real purpose: To help the grunt. It is unfortunate that many helicopters never had the opportunity to fulfill their one true mission in life, simply because someone forgot this fact.

41. If you have not been there and done that you probably will not understand most of these.

AS SEEN ON TV

Members of the Intelligence Community are as fascinated by their favorite TV shows as anyone else. One series that shows individuals with skills similar to what intelligence analysts do is the CSI trio, in which investigators try to piece together clues. The opening-scene bon mot of CSI: Miami that leads to The Who's "Eyaah!" lead to a contest in which authors had to write the opening setup, and Horatio Cane's three-part punch line. Among the contestants:

We arrested the 2nd Street Java barista for the murder, boss.
Now the only…thing she'll proudly serve…is hard time.

We found a screwdriver with the murderer's fingerprints on it.
Oh, really? Looks like this killer…is screwed.

Detective, the Greeks are assisting the Iranian nuclear program now.
Well, then. It looks like Iran needed…some gyros.

Why do you wear two pairs of glass all the time?
Well, I guess you could say…I know what sunglasses…are four!

Did you hear about all the animals for sale at NGA?

Could be…that I just…bought the Farm.

The killer got to Bieber before his concert.

Looks like the killer…was Justin time.

She was an Olympic archer. Ironic to be killed like this—with her own equipment.

It must have…been a very…arrowing way to die.

George Lucas just sold out to Disney!

Is it just me…or does this deal feel…Forced!?

We found the bodies at the rear of the ship.

That settles it! This killer…must be dealt with sternly.

After his routine, the comic tried to drown the victim in the toilet.

I never thought…he was much…of a commode-ian.

The killer cut up the body and labeled each part with a letter, but we cannot find the first one. This is madness!

Madness? No…this is PART A!

It looks like the Bath Salt Killer has struck again, H.

Hmmm. The vic's lack of face…disturbs me.

Looks like the Germans avoided the Maginot Line by going through the Ardennes!

Well…looks like the French…are fried.

We found this winning lottery ticket next to the body.

Is that right? Looks like the victim…forgot to cash in his last ticket.

Forensics suggests it was a set-up at the Tootsie factory.

Well, then. It looks like our vic…was a sucker.

We found the victim at the table with a half-eaten bowl of cereal and two .38 shots to the back of the head.

Well, snap…crackle…pop, pop!

…divorced. She's the prime suspect. Shame, bein' the holidays and all.

Yeah…he had a really…bad ex-miss.

This stiff raises the body count to a wizard, two elves, a dwarf, and now Frodo.

Looks like this guy…just turned murder…into a hobbit.

I don't know what happened, boss. We had all the exits covered.

Well, dang. I guess those were…the droids we were looking for.

The two vics were at the REM concert during the Mayan Apocalypse date, Cane.

Well, Frank. It's the end of the world as we know it…and I don't feel fine.

They say she was killed by a swarm of bees.

That's a heckuva…Honey Boo Boo.

Sir, the Congresswoman was able to wound her attacker…in the crotch.

Looks like…our killer…got sequestrated.

PHOTOCOPIER LORE

In the days before there was Reply-All and Forward in e-mail, there was the photocopied bit of humor, to be shared with your 400 closest friends. In 1999, these Basic Truths, Social Skills, and the PC Way to Say Things made the rounds. Many of the aphorisms went on to become popular bumper stickers and lapel pins.

Basic Truths:

Depression is merely anger without enthusiasm.

The early bird gets the worm, but the second mouse gets the cheese.

If you're not living on the edge, you're taking up too much space.

A little inaccuracy sometimes saves tons of explanation.

Indecision is the key to flexibility.

A penny saved is ridiculous.

The facts, although interesting, are usually irrelevant.

Friends may come and go, but enemies accumulate.

You can't have the real highs in life, without the deep lows.

If you can smile when things go wrong, you have someone in mind to blame.

Ambition is a poor excuse for not having enough sense to be lazy.

Success always occurs in private, and failure in full view. (*Ed's Note:* An item of faith with Agency folk, who keep their accomplishments quiet, so that the methods can be used downstream, while the press touts putative failures.)

A clear conscience is usually the sign of a bad memory.

No matter how much you do, you never do enough.

Hard work has a future payoff. Laziness pays off now.

Few women admit their age and few men act it.

He who hesitates is probably right.

Honesty is the best policy, but insanity is a better defense.

Even if you're on the right track, you'll get run over if you just sit there.

Think negative, and you've already failed.

Change is inevitable, except from a vending machine.

Reality's the only obstacle to happiness.

Dates on calendar are closer than they appear to be.

If you can't be kind, at least be vague.

Success in life is a long, hard climb.

Nothing is foolproof to a sufficiently talented fool.

It's better to keep one's mouth shut and appear stupid than open it and remove all doubts.

If you can't convince them, confuse them.

Pride is what we have. Vanity is what others have.

He who laughs last, always thinks the slowest.

Some people are alive only because it's illegal to kill them.

Some grow with responsibility, others just swell.

You never really learn to swear until you learn to drive.

Seen it all, done it all, can't remember most of it.

We all have a photographic memory. Some just don't have film.

The only way to get rid of temptation is to yield to it.

Health is merely the slowest possible rate at which one can die.

Social Skills:

Lie about trivial things such as the time of day.

Signal that a conversation is over by clamping your hands over your ears.

Drum on every available surface, or whistle obscure tunes.

Fill up shopping trolleys and leave them stranded at strategic locations.

Point a hairdryer at passing cars to see if they slow down.

only type in lower case and dont use punctuation

Pay for everything with small change.

Wave at strangers enthusiastically.

Invent computer jargon in conversations and see if people play along to avoid appearing stupid.

Stand over someone's shoulder, mumbling as they read.

Change channels constantly on the television for no reason.

Chew on borrowed pens.

Do not add any inflection to the end of sentences, producing awkward silences with the impression you'll be saying more at any moment.

Repeat everything a person says as a question.

Specify that your drive-through order is "to take-away" or "to go" for you Americans.

Contaminate the entire auto department of a store by sampling all of the spray air fresheners.

Adjust the color on the TV so that people appear green, and then insist that you like it that way.

Insist on keeping your car windshield wipers running in all weather conditions "to keep them tuned up".

Politically Correct Terms

Alive	temporarily metabolically abled
Dead	metabolically different
Ignorant	factually unencumbered
Bald	follicularly challenged
Poor	economically marginalized
Lazy	motivationally dispossessed
Dishonest	ethically disoriented
Homeless	residentially flexible
Addiction	pharmacological preference
Fat	alternative body image
Crazy	emotionally different
Old	chronologically gifted
Clumsy	uniquely coordinated
Psychopath	socially misaligned
Thief	ethically challenged
Rude	politically correct
Fart	gastronomic expression
Black	person of color
Female	person of gender
Minority group	under-represented population
Ugly	aesthetically challenged
Short	differently statured
Quiet person	conversational minimalist
Hearing person	temporarily aurally abled
Sighted person	temporarily visually abled
Pregnancy	parasitic oppression
Workaholic	recreationally challenged
Cook	food engineer
Baker	bread technician
Student	academic freak
Tone deaf	musically delayed
Caretaker	sanitation engineer
Paper bag	processed tree carcass

Another popular photocopied item compared the Cook County Correctional Center in Chicago, Illinois, with the Pentagon, observing "just in case you ever get these two environments mixed up, this comparison chart should make things a little bit clearer:

@prison: You spend most of your time in a 10x10 cell
@work: You spend most of your time in a 6x6 cubicle

@prison: You get three fully paid-for meals a day.
@work: You get a break for one meal, and you have to pay for it.

@prison: For good behavior, you get time off.
@work: For good behavior, you get more work.

@prison: The guard locks and unlocks all the doors for you.
@work: You must carry a security card and open all the doors yourself.

@prison: You can watch TV and play games.
@work: You could get fired for watching TV and playing games.

@prison: You get your own toilet.
@work: You have to share the toilet with people who pee on the seat.

@prison: They allow your family and friends to visit.
@work: You aren't even supposed to speak to your family.

@prison: All expenses are paid by the taxpayers with no work required on your part.
@work: You must pay all your expenses to go to work, and they deduct taxes from your salary to pay for prisoners.

@prison: You spend most of your life inside bars wanting to get out.
@work: You spent most of your time wanting to get out and go inside bars.

@prison: You must deal with sadistic wardens.
@work: They are called "Generals".

There is something seriously wrong with this picture. Now get back to work. You're not getting paid to check e-mails!

Ten Unwritten Rules of Engineering

1. If it's stupid but it works, it's not stupid.
2. If it's working but you still think it's stupid, see Rule #1.
3. "Perfect" is the enemy of "good enough".
4. The amount of time needed to get anything fielded will rarely be based on proper engineering principles.
5. Design requirements are like food and water; you can live without them for a short time, but eventually your project will die unless you get them.
6. Every engineering process has to deal with "requirements creep". Just make sure that "creep" doesn't turn into "flat out run".
7. It doesn't qualify as "man portable" if it requires four large men and a small boy to carry it.
8. There is rarely a single right solution, but there are multiple wrong ones.
9. If you think the user interface is unimportant, then ask yourself why Apple products are so popular.
10. Stay married to your spouse, not to the idea of "this is absolutely the way it needs to be built".

// 🌐 //

Intelligence officers often meld their style of writing with fictional or current affairs events. WikiLeaks, otherwise a major headache for the IC, came in for such treatment:

WookieLeaks

1. Despite billions invested on construction of an untested defense system, the new Death Star may not yet be fully operational.
2. We're never going to be able to do planet-building on a place like Endor. %^&ing backwards Ewoks don't even want us there.
3. Protocol droid fluent in 6 million languages discharged for violating DADT.
4. "Professional" rebel fighters cannot figure out whether it's a trap; a walking calamari had to tell them.
5. Trillions in Imperial war funds have been ending up in the pockets of private bounty hunter guilds! Taxpayers got what?

6. Admiral Ackbar emails peppered with casual anti-semitism, anti-jawaism.
7. Inquiry reveals cantina footage digitally altered; Han Solo discharged weapon first.
8. The Jedi cult harbors secret beliefs of taking midichlorian readings with e-meters and worshipping the shots of Jedi Masters.
9. Critics say that #wookieleaks undermines Emperor's "Death Start" strategy.
10. Empire leaders reported to accept captives in exchange for "looking the other way" re: illegal gas mining activities.

// 🌐 //

Bin Laden's Last Facebook posting:

Osama Bin Laden
BRB Someone's at the door
Tuesday at 04:00
US Navy SEALS like this.

// 🌐 //

One of my favorite items from the International Spy Museum is the **Top 10 Reasons I Didn't Make it in the CIA**, available as refrigerator magnets, t-shirts, and other paraphernalia:

#10. I talk in my sleep.
#9 I'm open to bribes.
#8 I thought Cloak & Dagger was a rock group.
#7 My license to kill was suspended.
#6 When I heard there was a leak, I called a plumber.
#5 My favorite dead drop site is a trash can.
#4 My letter of recommendation is from bin Laden.
#3 I asked which office Jack Bauer works in.
#2 I filled out application in invisible ink.
#1 I thought I was applying to Culinary Institute of America.

// 🌐 //

In the early 2010s, Internet social media sites were replete with six-photo caption contests purporting to describe various groups' perceptions of one's activities. DI analysts offered the following interpretation of how they are seen:

What my friends think I do (poster of Annie from Covert Affairs)

What my parents think I do (poster of Jack Ryan in The Hunt for Red October, Patriot Games, Clear and Present Danger)

What policymakers think I do (poster of Chicken Little movie)

What my boss thinks I do (Shakespeare writing with a quill pen)

What I think I do (photo of President Obama meeting with 3 key advisors)

What I actually do (still from cubicle drone from Office Space)

A FEW GRATUITOUS JACK BAUER OBSERVATIONS

The Agency and 24's Jack Bauer, peace be upon him, have little in common other than saving the world before breakfast. Many Agency officers, however, enjoyed the series and the movie, although many think that the movie should have been called 2.

Here's a sample of some of the humor that was passed around the Agency regarding the show's hero, much of it originally collected by http://www.notrly.com/jackbauer/index.php?

Jack Bauer once stepped into quicksand. The quicksand couldn't escape and nearly drowned.

Jack Bauer doesn't breathe. The air hides in his lungs for protection.

If a tree falls in the forest, it's because Jack Bauer wants it down.

Jack Bauer can start a fire using only water.

Jack Bauer makes onions cry.

Jack Bauer beat the sun in a staring contest.

The city of Los Angeles once named a street after Jack Bauer in gratitude for his saving the city several times. They had to rename it after people kept dying when they tried to cross the street. No one crosses Jack Bauer and lives.

If you are still verbally capable of telling Jack Bauer that he is hurting you, then trust me, he isn't.

Chloe O'Brien's real last name is Dammit.

There are two hands that can beat a royal flush. Jack Bauer's right hand and Jack Bauer's left hand.

Jack Bauer was once charged with attempted murder in Los Angeles County, but the judge dropped all charges because Jack Bauer never "attempts" murder.

If Jack Bauer had been a Spartan the movie would have been called "1".

It takes you 24 weeks just to watch what Jack Bauer does in a single day.

Most people would need months to recover from 20 months of Chinese interrogation. Jack Bauer needs a shower, a shave and a change of clothes.

Some people see the glass as half full. Others see it as half empty. Jack Bauer sees the glass as a deadly weapon.

Jack Bauer never retreats; he just attacks in the opposite direction.

When a convicted terrorist was sentenced to face Jack Bauer, he appealed to have the sentence reduced to death.

Withholding information from Jack Bauer is now classified as a suicide attempt.

When bad things happen to good people, it's probably fate. When bad things happen to bad people, it's probably Jack Bauer.

Once, someone tried to tell Jack Bauer a "knock knock" joke. Jack Bauer found out who was there, who they worked for, and where the goddamned bomb was.

Jack Bauer once showed up late for work. CTU adjusted their clocks accordingly. (*Ed's note:* Jack Bauer led the Counter Terrorist Unit.)

If Jack Bauer gives you his word that you'll get your deal, then he really means it. Unless you killed David Palmer. Then you're dead.

On a high school math test, Jack Bauer put down "Violence" as every one of the answers. He got an A+ on the test because Jack Bauer solves all his problems with Violence.

Jack Bauer always tests positive for steroids. Not that he uses steroids. It's because steroids are made from Jack Bauer.

On Jack Bauer's tax returns, he has to claim the entire world as his dependents.

There are three leading causes of death among terrorists. The first two are Jack Bauer, and the third one is heart attack from hearing Jack Bauer is coming for them.

The only prerequisite to becoming a CTU security guard is being able to accept being rendered unconscious by Jack Bauer.

When Jack Bauer was told smiling increases your face value, he said not speaking increases your life span.

Jack Bauer doesn't laugh in the face of danger; Jack Bauer is the face of danger.

If everyone on "24" followed Jack Bauer's instructions, it would be called "12".

Jack Bauer definitely loves his daughter; he wouldn't let anyone else who made that many stupid decisions live.

If Jack Bauer was in a room with Hitler, Stalin, and Nina Meyers, and he had a gun with 2 bullets, he'd shoot Nina twice.

Passed out, surrounded by terrorists and nerve gas, and handcuffed to a table leg, Jack Bauer laughed to himself and said, "I have them right where I want them."

Jack Bauer quit for just five minutes, and a nuclear bomb went off.

At Jack Bauer's funeral, there will be a eulogy, twenty-gun salute, and a squadron of F-14s flying over the procession. All of which will be performed by Jack Bauer.

When someone asked Jack Bauer if he was afraid of James Bond, he replied "What does 'afraid' mean?"

If Jack Bauer was president, he would protect the Secret Service.

Torturing terrorists is like riding a bike. Jack Bauer never forgets.

Professor Charles Xavier from X-Men once tried to read Jack Bauer's mind. Now he's sitting in a wheel chair.

There have been no terrorist attacks in the US since Jack Bauer appeared on television.

The Supreme Court ruled unanimously that Jack Bauer's methods were "cruel and unusual punishment". The next day the Supreme Court had nine vacancies.

Jack Bauer doesn't take fingerprints, he takes fingers.

Superman's only weakness is Kryptonite. Jack Bauer laughs at Superman for having a weakness.

Jack Bauer once won a game of Connect 4 in 3 moves.

If Jack Bauer gives you his word, return it immediately and run.

Jack Bauer is the leading cause of death in Middle Eastern men.

In order to control illegal immigration in the United States, the president installed cardboard cutouts of Jack Bauer along the US/Mexico border.

When the president runs out of options he says: "Get me Jack Bauer, immediately."

A standard deck now contains 48 cards. Too many people were getting hurt for trying to play Jack.

The only reason the Chinese kept Jack alive is so that he could bring down the population.

Jack Bauer was never addicted to heroin. Heroin was addicted to Jack Bauer.

The first words spoken after the Big Bang were, "The following takes place between the birth of Jack Bauer and eternity."

Jack Bauer teaches a course at Harvard entitled: "Time Management: Making the Most Out Of Each Day."

RIP Edgar If you see this give it a 10. Just cuz it's what Edgar would have wanted. :(

When Special Forces raided an Afghan training camp, they found an empty camp and a pirated copy of 24 Season 4.

Jack Bauer does not need to use a silencer... he just tells his gun to be quiet.

"Jack Bauer Camp" makes "Guantanamo Bay" sound like a weekend retreat in the Hamptons.

Jack Bauer is currently involved in a complex law suit with the California Department of Justice due to their attempt to ban Jack Bauer as an "Assault Weapon". Jack maintains he is primarily used for hunting and target shooting, and is quite safe to have around families. But statistics don't lie.

When Jack Bauer goes to the airport and the metal detector doesn't go off, security gives him a gun.

When Jack Bauer took a stress test, the test failed.

There is the right way, the wrong way, and the Jack Bauer way. It's basically the right way, but faster and with more deaths.

Jack Bauer once acted as judge, jury, and executioner; but to save time he now just acts as executioner.

The next fiscal year's budget for the US Military covers Jack Bauer, two pistols and four billion rounds of ammunition.

There is a deeper reason that Kim will not forgive Jack. For years during her birthday and Christmas when Kim would look for presents Jack would just laugh to himself before finally telling her, "I give you my word."

When Jack Bauer ran out of ammo, he caught 3 bullets in his chest and used them to reload.

Jack Bauer broke into the Russian Consulate and got captured because he thought it would be fun to compare Russian prisons with Chinese prisons.

Jack Bauer's calendar goes from March 31 to April 2. No one fools Jack Bauer.

If a suspect mentions your name, while being interrogated by Jack Bauer, you have a 3.26% chance of surviving the next 3 hours.

Jack Bauer doesn't have a refresh button on his web browser. All events take place in real time.

Jack Bauer once forgot where he put his keys. He then spent the next half-hour torturing himself until he gave up the location of the keys.

If you park your car illegally in a handicapped space and Jack Bauer catches you, you won't ever have to park illegally again.

The United States government implemented Daylight Savings Time because Jack Bauer requested more overtime.

Jack Bauer can type 90 words per minute. On his cell phone.

Jack Bauer can order a Big Mac at Burger King.

Jack Bauer sends an ambulance after he shoots your innocent wife above the kneecap. Jack Bauer has morals.

If Jack Bauer was interrogating Morpheus in "The Matrix", Zion would have been dead.

There is only one rule for dating Jack Bauer's daughter. Don't.

The grass is always greener on the other side, unless Jack Bauer has been there. In that case the grass is most likely soaked in blood and tears.

To Jack Bauer, Level 8 Security just means it takes 8 seconds to infiltrate.

Many beautiful women ask Jack Bauer to sleep with them on a daily basis but he always refuses. Is it because he's gay? No, it's because Jack Bauer doesn't sleep.

Every time Jack Bauer yells "NOW!" at the end of a sentence, a terrorist dies.

China is now the number one importer of weapons of mass destruction: Jack Bauer.

There are two things you can always count on: Death and Jack Bauer causing it.

Jack Bauer brings a knife to a gun fight and always wins.

When Jack Bauer calls shotgun, he means it.

Jack Bauer puts the rage in courage.

Jack Bauer can sneeze with his eyes open.

By seizing Jack Bauer, China has jumped to #1 in the world for the quality of weaponry available in inventory.

When Jack takes his knife out, the terror alert level automatically drops to green.

The reason why terrorists attacked New York City was because Jack Bauer was in LA.

"The valley of the shadow of death", refers to anywhere within a 25 mile radius of Jack Bauer.

Jack Bauer once won a game of rock paper scissors using neither rock, paper, nor scissors.

Kim Bauer once brought her father to school for a parent/teacher conference.....and got expelled for bringing a weapon onto school grounds.

Jack Bauer does not use birth control. He simply demands that you not get pregnant.

Jack Bauer once climbed Mount Everest. While at the summit, the President called him with an urgent message. He was back at CTU Los Angeles in 15 minutes.

Only Jack Bauer can get more information out of his interrogator than the interrogator gets out of him.

Most children slept with a teddy bear and blanket when they were young, Jack Bauer did the same thing but with a real bear.

Jack Bauer doesn't have a middle name. Nothing gets between Jack Bauer.

If you run away from Jack Bauer, you're just gonna die tired.

Jack Bauer found out they were making a 24 video game, and killed the makers. No one plays Jack Bauer.

In the short time Jack Bauer was dead, he tortured the Devil and found the secret to immortality....and before he left hell to come back to life, he bitch slapped Nina Myers one last time.

If you have a headache, it's because Jack Bauer is thinking about you.

Jack Bauer never needs to wear a raincoat. Rain knows better than to fall on Jack Bauer.

For every result you get during a Google search, Jack Bauer tortured someone to get it up there.

Killing Jack Bauer doesn't make him dead. It just makes him angry.

If you wake up in the morning, it's because Jack Bauer spared your life.

1.6 billion Chinese are angry with Jack Bauer. Sounds like a fair fight.

Jack Bauer played Russian Roulette with a fully loaded gun and won.

When life gave Jack Bauer lemons, he used them to kill terrorists. Jack Bauer hates lemonade.

Al Qaeda's recent proposal for truce is a direct result of them finding out that Jack Bauer is, in fact, still alive.

When Jack Bauer was a child, he made his mother finish his vegetables.

Simon Says should be renamed to Jack Bauer Says because if Jack Bauer says something then you better do it.

Jack Bauer won the Tour de France on a unicycle to prove to Lance Armstrong it wasn't a big deal. He thinks yellow wristbands are gay.

When Jack Bauer pisses into the wind, the wind changes direction.

Jack Bauer's favorite color is severe terror alert red. His second favorite color is violet, but just because it sounds like violent.

When you open a can of whoop-ass, Jack Bauer jumps out.

When Google can't find something, it asks Jack Bauer for help.

You can lead a horse to water. Jack Bauer can make him drink.

When the boogie man goes to sleep, he checks his closet for Jack Bauer.

When Jack Bauer was a child his parents threw him a surprise birthday party. ONCE.

Upon finding David Palmer's dead body, Jack Bauer resurrected him from the dead, trained him to become a special forces soldier, strategically placed him in a group known simply as "the Unit" and moved him to another network.

The only time Jack Bauer looks Death in the eye is when he's looking in a mirror.

After having sex with your wife, apologize for not being Jack Bauer.

Insurance applications are now required by law to ask: "Are you a friend of Jack Bauer?"

Jack Bauer does not watch breaking news, he breaks the news.

Swiss cheese didn't used to have holes in it until Jack Bauer thought it was a terrorist.

Jack Bauer knows where the cast of Lost is.

When Jack Bauer was a baby, he took candy from adults.

When you get a collect call from Jack Bauer, the operator doesn't even bother to ask if you accept the charges.

Jack Bauer's cell phone battery died 12 years ago. It has run on pure adrenaline ever since.

50 million people can't be wrong; unless Jack Bauer says so.

Jack Bauer fought Cancer. Now it's safe to smoke.

Jack Bauer went on Who Wants to be a Millionaire? only so he could phone a friend and yell, "You're running out of time!" for 30 seconds.

If Jack Bauer shoots you, it's because he has a plan. If you live, you're part of that plan.

Jack Bauer and Dr. Gregory House are good friends. As soon as Jack kills a man, House saves him so that Jack can kill him again.

Who says Jack Bauer does not have a heart? He's holding one in his hand right now.

If Jack Bauer doesn't kill you on the first shot, he is trying to torture you.

The Army stopped recruiting when they realized Jack Bauer was in fact the army.

Jack Bauer doesn't get morning wood. He gets morning steel. Stainless steel.

In Season 6, Episode 4, Jack didn't actually see a nuclear flash. That was God telling Jack to man up.

Jack Bauer can tell a book by its cover.

There are two kinds of people in the world. Those who fear Jack Bauer, and those who are Jack Bauer.

The last time Jack Bauer got angry…Germany surrendered.

Jack Bauer can make you remember things you never knew.

The rules of poker have recently been revised. Now the winning hand is the one with the most Jacks in it.

Jack Bauer doesn't aim. He tells bullets where to go.

When he was a kid, Jack Bauer didn't play "red light, green light". Every light is green for Jack Bauer.

Jack Bauer cannot stick his elbow in his ear, but he can stick your elbow in your ear.

Commissioner Gordon only rings the Batphone when he cannot get Jack Bauer on the Bauerphone.

When Jack Bauer tells you to jump, you don't ask "How high?" You ask "when can I come down?"

Jack Bauer can slam rotating doors.

Chuck Norris wears a bear to hide the scar that Jack Bauer gave him.

Jack Bauer once beat Mona Lisa in a staring contest.

Looks can only kill if Jack Bauer is looking at you.

Jack Bauer refused the key to the city of Los Angeles. He figured he could pick the lock anyway.

Jack Bauer once killed 183 men with one bullet. Without a gun.

Despite being white, Jack Bauer was admitted into the Black Panthers. Not only because of his amazing ability, but also because his name rhymes with Black Power.

Jack Bauer once bowled a 301.

Jack Bauer had phone sex with a woman and got her pregnant.

Water can go only three days without Jack Bauer.

It took Andy Dufresne 20 years to tunnel out of Shawshank Prison. It took Jack Bauer five minutes, four of which were spent torturing Warren Norton.

Jack Bauer killed Kenny.

You're going to tell Jack Bauer what he wants to know; it's just a question of how much you want it to hurt.

Jack Bauer does not use doors. He makes his own.

Jack Bauer shaves the sights off his guns; they get in his way when he's trying to shoot.

Nike doesn't show Jack Bauer advertisements because they know he'll "do it" when he's goddamn ready.

Jack Bauer laughs at the movie Mission Impossible. There is no impossible mission for Jack.

Jack Bauer has a can of whoop-ass for cologne.

Jack Bauer's favorite air freshener scent is "vanilla napalm".

Once time when Jack Bauer was a kid, he invoked Section 112 Protocol, overwriting his parent's authority. He made them go to their rooms for 2 hours. They stayed for 3.

There are only two types of people in the world:

- Those who will do anything for Jack, and will eventually die as a result.
- Those who are secretly plotting to betray Jack, and who will eventually die as a result.

Jack Bauer has single-handedly popularized messenger bags for straight men.

If there is one thing Jack Bauer hates as much as terrorists, it's protocol.

Killing Jack Bauer doesn't make him dead. It just makes him angry.

If Jack says, "I just want to talk to him/her" and that him/her is you, well, amigo, you're dead.

Jack Bauer's hands are illegal in every state except for one: the State of Emergency.

Jack Bauer once played 18 holes of golf and shot a 17.

Jack Bauer got in a car accident and protected his air bag.

Instead of buzzing, Jack Bauer's alarm clock screams out, "There's no more time!"

Jack Bauer turns his regular bathtub into a Jacuzzi simply by intimidating the water until it begins trembling in fear.

Jack Bauer has killed more men than he has spoken to.

Instead of tickling Elmo, Jack Bauer shot him.

Jack Bauer once killed a group of Samurai Warriors with only a ball-point pen, which led to the phrase "The pen is mightier than the sword."

If you're a passenger in the car that Jack Bauer is driving and he gets a call from the President, ask to be let out at the corner. Somebody is going to die.

Jack Bauer can talk about what happens in Vegas outside of Vegas.

All video games now feature four difficulty levels: easy, normal, hard, and Jack Bauer... No one has ever beaten the game on Jack Bauer.

Jack Bauer can make Chloe smile.

Jack Bauer is not thankful for each day. Each day is thankful for Jack Bauer.

A "Bauer movement" is when you wet yourself after Jack Bauer shows up at your door.

When Big Tobacco claimed that cigarettes didn't cause cancer in test subjects, the test subjects were all Jack Bauer.

Justin Gatlin tied the 100m world record this year because Jack Bauer was chasing him.

Wayne Gretzky is "The Great One" because Jack Bauer does not play hockey.

Jack Bauer doesn't need to carry an umbrella. He dodges raindrops.

Jack Bauer told Chloe that she was the best computer tech in the world, then told her something she didn't know about computers.

If Jack Bauer had been in The Terminator, Arnold would have never been back.

Jack Bauer saved Private Ryan.

The number one cause of death in America is heart disease. The number one cause of heart disease is fear of Jack Bauer.

Jack Daniels drinks Jack Bauer. Daniels then suffers a 24-hour hangover.

Quentin Tarantino finds Jack Bauer too violent.

When Neo and Jack Bauer fought, Jack shot him. Nobody dodges Jack Bauer's bullets.

Jack Bauer's influence is so strong that with one call to the NCAA, the former director of CTU, George Mason, was able to make it to the Final Four.

Statistically, the most dangerous occupations in America are logger, pilot, fisherman, and knowing Jack Bauer is alive.

When Jack shot Victor Drazen eight times, it wasn't because he was irritated, it was because he wanted to see how many shots he could get off before Victor hit the water.

If you shoot Jack Bauer in a dream, you'd better wake up and apologize to him.

Jack Bauer's file says he was the commander of Special Forces after being in the Army for 20 years. In truth, he was the Army's Special Forces for 20 years, but he wanted a new challenge after he toppled the USSR.

In an average living room there are 1,242 objects Jack Bauer can use to kill you, including the room itself.

Jack Bauer's parents taught him hide and seek at age 4. They are still trying to find him.

Creators of the 24 video game were shocked to find that everyone who played the game wound up getting shot above the knee. Nobody pushes Jack Bauer's buttons.

For his 40th birthday, Jack Bauer wished that Nina Myers was alive, so he could kill her again.

Every time the cops get an APB to arrest Jack Bauer, half the department mysteriously calls out sick. The fire department, too, just in case. (*Ed's note:* APB: All Points Bulletin.)

Jack Bauer has never had a beer in a bar. Chloe always uploads it to his PDA.

Jack Bauer once played Pictionary blind folded and still ended up killing eight terrorists.

When Jack Bauer asks for your help, he's not asking.

James Bond's "License to Kill" was given to him by Jack Bauer.

Jack won with rock even when paper covered him. No one can cover Jack Bauer.

It was once believed that Jack Bauer actually lost a fight to a terrorist, but it was a lie, created by Jack to lure more terrorists to him. Terrorists never were very smart.

When you walk into a bar and Jack Bauer's your wingman, you're not probably gonna get laid. You will get laid.

If Jack Bauer smoked marijuana, it would be legal.

Never bring Jack Bauer into your home. You will be arrested for possession of a weapon of mass destruction.

Jack Bauer doesn't need money. "I give you my word" is enough.

Jack Bauer did not hire clowns for Kim's birthday parties. He stood in front of the children and demanded that they enjoy themselves.

When Jack Bauer goes to donate blood, he declines the syringe, and instead requests a hand gun and a bucket.

Jack Bauer didn't pull the wings off flies when he was a child. He pulled the arms off the boys who pulled the wings off flies.

Jack Bauer got to level 71 on Tetris. Blindfolded.

If you look up terrorist in the dictionary you will not see Jack Bauer, but Jack Bauer will see you.

When Jack Bauer says he sees dead people, he's serious, because he killed them.

Jack Bauer doesn't need to memorize his PIN number. He just tells the ATM machine, "You're gonna give me $60 in 20s. It's just a matter of how much you want it to hurt."

Jack Bauer can eat just one Lay's potato chip.

It would take the entire teams of CSI Las Vegas, Miami, and New York to process a crime scene where Jack Bauer was responsible for the body count.

Jack Bauer can beat the gay out of Elton John.

Jack Bauer is the reason Jason Bourne cannot remember anything. Bourne should consider himself lucky he does not remember Jack.

Chinese prison was a vacation for Jack Bauer. It was the first time he could actually sleep, eat, and go to the bathroom.

A black cat crossed Jack Bauer's path and was promptly hit by a car.

Congress authorized the printing of a 24 dollar bill with Jack Bauer's picture on it, but the printing machines broke under the stress of his awesomeness.

On Halloween, Jack Bauer always has candy because no one tricks Jack Bauer.

Jack Bauer's death was not staged. Jack came back to life after Satan was scared to let him into Hell.

Henderson's men actually took cover behind a water tank. Unfortunately, when Jack Bauer wants an explosion, water turns into natural gas.

Colin Farrell smokes a pack of cigarettes a day. Jack Bauer smokes a pack of terrorists any time he feels like it.

Jack Bauer plays dodge ball with a bowling ball.

The producers of 24 force Jack Bauer to use a stunt double. Not to ensure his safety, but to ensure the safety of the set and its actors.

Jack Bauer doesn't follow the "Don't ask, don't tell" policy. Bauer asks, you'd better tell. Or else.

There are no natural disasters in California. Except for earthquakes. This is because the earth trembles in fear of Jack Bauer.

Jack Bauer's only kidding. He knows whom you're working for.

Dirty Harry once told Jack Bauer to "Make my day." Seen any new Dirty Harry movies lately?

Jack Bauer doesn't need a bulletproof vest. He only wears one to protect the bullets.

The State of the Union Address was originally scheduled for Monday but Jack Bauer made the President change it to Tuesday.

Jack Bauer doesn't think in terms of right and wrong, just "what I'm going to do" and "why the hell are you slowing me down?"

Jack Bauer's first job was as a waiter, but he was fired soon after. Jack Bauer takes orders from no one.

Jack Bauer walked into traffic and killed 3 cars.

Whoever said "You can't win 'em all" obviously wasn't talking to Jack Bauer.

Kobe would pass to Jack Bauer.

A bird in the hand is worth two in the bush. Unless the bird is in Jack Bauer's hand. Then that bird is dead.

Jehovah's Witnesses skip Jack Bauer's house.

Jack Bauer once found the cure for cancer. He destroyed it immediately, but then realized that cancer was the only thing giving him competition in the Deaths per Day category.

The CTU LA Employee of the Month has been eliminated since Jack Bauer came around. They now have an Employee of the Hour, and Bauer has won all but one of those awards. RIP George Mason.

Back Bauer is allowed to leave his phone on during a movie.

Jack Bauer doesn't tie his shoelaces. He points a gun at his shoes and dares them to fall off.

At work Jack Bauer squeezes grenades, necks and triggers. Stress balls are for pussies.

Sony had Jack Bauer beta test the 24 video game. As soon as he had Chloe widen the parameters, the game was beaten in 60 minutes.

The Fantastic Four are being sued to change their name. Jack Bauer's knuckles are the real Fantastic Four.

In 6th grade, Jack Bauer refused to play dodge ball. Jack Bauer only plays hardball.

Die Hard is the funniest movie Jack Bauer's ever seen.

Jack Bauer once donated blood to a hospital. The doctors realized that no one could ever receive Jack Bauer's blood directly. They had to do something with it, though. This is why we now have steroids.

Contrary to popular belief, the clock noise on 24 isn't recorded. It's a live feed from Jack Bauer's heart.

The opening scene of Saving Private Ryan is loosely based on games of dodge ball that Jack Bauer played in second grade.

While most children were playing Cops and Robbers, Jack Bauer was playing Jack Bauer and Robbers. Those men are still in jail today.

Kim Bauer's dad can beat up your dad.

Jack Bauer doesn't need a map. All roads lead to Jack Bauer.

While being "put under" in the hospital, Jack Bauer can count backwards from 100 every time. This annoys the doctors.

David Palmer did not get that horrible burn on his hand from a biological agent. He got it after he high-fived Jack.

We call it "Girls Gone Wild". Jack Bauer calls it "whenever Jack Bauer enters a room".

Jack Bauer spends an hour each morning practicing saying "NOW!"

The government takes portions of Jack Bauer's lungs to make gas masks.

Jack Bauer is the only reason Santa Claus is able to deliver presents to millions of children in a 24-hour period.

If you break one of Jack Bauer's ribs, he'll just use it to stab you to death.

Scissors are scared to run with Jack Bauer.

The Department of Homeland Security's threat advisory (e.g., red = severe) is really a measurement of how ticked off Jack Bauer is.

Jack Bauer's favorite reality show is 24.

Jack Bauer doesn't cry. The man you see is his "emotion double".

The Angel of Death has Jack Bauer on speed dial.

Jack Bauer won the Indy 500 in a Ford Explorer.

Police label anyone attacking Jack Bauer as a Code 45-11…a suicide.

Those guys on Prison Break should give up. Jack Bauer will only hunt them down next season.

Jack Bauer didn't do heroin for the feeling. He just wanted to make sure he can kill terrorists in any situation. He can.

Jack Bauer doesn't swim in shark-infested waters because it wouldn't be fair to them.

During the childhood game "Duck, Duck, Goose", no one "goosed" Jack Bauer. Ever.

Life is all fun and games. Unless Jack Bauer finds you playing it. Then it's game over.

Oxygen requires Jack Bauer to survive.

Superman once hid behind Jack Bauer in a firefight.

If the show was called Bauer: Texas Ranger, the show would still be in production.

Chuck Norris once roundhouse kicked Jack Bauer in the face. Jack blinked.

Consenting to be Jack Bauer's partner automatically makes your life insurance null and void.

The quickest way to the endangered species list is Jack Bauer.

The Devil sold his soul to Jack Bauer.

In God we trust, but God trusts Jack Bauer.

The most valuable thing in the world is Jack Bauer's word. If Jack Bauer gives you his word, you can go to the bank and take out a $10,000,000 loan, no questions asked.

They should change CTU to CBU: Counting on Bauer Unit.

In Season 3, Ramon Salazar said "Jack Bauer has more lives than a cat." Untrue. Cats only live once.

Daylight Savings Time was created to give Jack Bauer an extra hour one day each year with which to kill terrorists.

If Jack Bauer were to fall into the ocean, he would not get wet, the ocean would get Jacked.

Deathly afraid of Jack Bauer, Minute Rice will fully cook itself in 15 seconds.

The term "power hour" has been replaced by "Bauer hour".

The French surrendered to Jack Bauer. Twice.

If Jack Bauer told you to stop reading this, you would stop reading this.

Jack Bauer can watch a nuclear explosion without suffering retinal damage.

Jack Bauer's high school counselor told him to "shoot for the stars". Jack Bauer has now destroyed over 1,216 stars using only a pistol.

If you shoot Jack Bauer, you better believe he will interrogate your bullet, and he'd know who shot at him.

Jack Bauer once made a blind man see again, then promptly threatened to cut out his eyes if he didn't give him the information he wanted.

Jack Bauer once lost his TV remote, but managed to regain control by calmly telling the television what to do.

The US government does not cover up the existence of aliens, they cover up the fact that Jack Bauer killed them all.

Sliced bread is the best thing since Jack Bauer.

Jack Bauer refused the Godfather's offer.

Before Austin 3:16 and John 3:16, there was Jack 3:16: "You will tell me what I need to know. It's just a matter of how much you want it to hurt." (*Ed's note:* Austin 3:16: A reference to pro wrestler Stone Cold Steve Austin.)

Jack Bauer didn't invent fear, but he does hold the patent.

Jack Bauer doesn't follow protocol. Protocol follows Jack Bauer.

Why did the terrorist cross the street? To get hit by a car before Jack Bauer could get him.

Every day is the longest day of Jack Bauer's life. For terrorists, the shortest.

If Jack Bauer were in Rocky VI, there would be no Rocky VII.

Jack Bauer was only wrong once, and that was when he thought he was wrong, but he was actually right.

The last man on Earth will be Jack Bauer, only because he has run out of people to kill.

It only took 3 minutes for Jack Bauer to find out Victoria's secret.

Jack Bauer once took part in a rodeo. He won it by throwing the bull.

75% of the Earth is covered by water. The other 25% is covered by Jack Bauer.

In honor of Jack Bauer's saving Los Angeles for the 5th straight season, Kobe Bryant changed his jersey number from 8 to 24.

One time, at band camp, Jack Bauer killed a guy with a flute.

The Butterfly Effect was originally going to star Jack Bauer, but they realized there was nothing to go back in time and correct.

Did you know that there was a national disaster last night while you were sleeping? Of course you didn't; Jack Bauer was on duty.

Only Jack Bauer can be reinstated on a provisional basis four times.

Whenever your significant other uses the line "It's not you, it's me", it was really Jack Bauer.

Jack Bauer once thought he'd saved the world with 61 seconds to spare. Then he found his watch was a minute fast.

Jack Bauer went to the Bermuda Triangle once. It disappeared.

Jack Bauer's Tic Tacs don't make noise in his pocket.

Every time someone gets their butt kicked, Jack Bauer gets a royalty.

Jack Bauer is Achilles without heels.

Normal people have trouble killing two birds with one stone. Jack Bauer killed 13 birds simultaneously with a dull pencil.

The sole ob of the Verizon wireless "can you hear me now" guy is to make sure Jack Bauer has cell phone reception. The fate of the US and all of the world depends upon it.

In the event of a crash your corpse doubles as Jack Bauer's flotation device.

The Seinfeld Soup Nazi gives Jack Bauer extra crackers.

Jack Bauer didn't invent torture; he perfected it.

Jack Bauer rents videos and never rewinds them, ever.

Jack Bauer prefers windows. Doors are for women, children, and people he throws through them.

If Jack Bauer wants to have a minute alone with you…well, basically you're dead.

If Jack Bauer forgets to spring ahead for Daylight Savings Time, time itself will simply stop while Jack catches up.

The earth rotates because it's trying to run from Jack Bauer.

Jack Bauer can get 24 in Blackjack and still win. Jack doesn't bust until he feels like it.

When you come face to face with Jack Bauer, you can do things the easy way or the hard way. The easy way is ingesting your cyanide pill.

Jack Bauer managed to get a second bag of peanuts from the flight attendant, although the airline does not serve peanuts.

Jack Bauer doesn't walk. The ground under him moves.

In second grade, Jack Bauer sent the teacher to the principal's office.

Jack Bauer found and killed the last 0.1% of odor-causing bacteria.

Jack Bauer, cashing in on his super-power ability to get to anywhere in L.A. in 15 minutes, is the employee of the month at Domino's...for 15 years straight.

Jeff Gordon drives Car 24 in NASCAR races because he hopes at least a few drivers think it's being driven by Jack Bauer and will drop out of the races.

Jack Bauer tortures foreigners into speaking in English.

Jack Bauer can take two years off from CTU and still remember all his access codes, because they know better than to change them while he's gone.

Jack Bauer gets five downs.

Jack Bauer never gets sick because his immune system is almost as deadly as he is.

Jack Bauer rolled a 13 playing craps in Vegas.

Jack Bauer did not pledge a fraternity in college, a fraternity pledged Jack Bauer.

Just because Jack Bauer shows up with jumper cables, doesn't mean someone called Triple A.

The Bird Flu almost made it to the US. Luckily Jack Bauer was there to shoot and kill it.

Jack refuses to play the lottery. It just wouldn't be fair to the millions of other players.

Jack Bauer gave a new meaning to the expression "break a leg" because he does it to several people every day.

Two heads are better than one, unless that one head is Jack Bauer's head.

Jack Bauer Syndrome isn't an illness, it's a cause of death.

The only time the terror alert level goes above "severe" is when Jack Bauer is crying.

It's no coincidence that Jack Bauer rhymes with power.

Anytime, anywhere, anyone shoots someone in the thigh, they have to pay a royalty to Jack Bauer.

The price is always right for Jack Bauer.

Jack Bauer hates casual conversation. He prefers bullets.

Jack Bauer can checkmate without moving his pawns.

Jack Bauer stole the cookie from the cookie jar. And then he shot you for asking him about it.

Jack Bauer knows what is in the secret sauce.

Jack Bauer was almost infected with the AIDS virus. Instead he gave AIDS Ebola.

Jack Bauer does not have to look both ways when he crosses the street.

Jack Bauer got an upgrade to first class even though the airplane did not have a first class section.

Jack Bauer entered a building swarming with 167 agents, all of them with orders to treat him as a hostile. Jack outnumbered them again.

The easy button is simply a metaphor to send Jack Bauer to eliminate a terrorist threat.

Jack Bauer once killed a room full of people because nobody blessed him when he sneeze.

When you feel like someone's watching you, it's Jack Bauer about to break your neck.

A watched pot doesn't boil unless Jack Bauer is doing the watching.

Jack Bauer invented a time machine for a 7th grade science fair. Why else do you think dinosaurs are extinct?

Jack Bauer is better at killing terrorists than suicide bombers.

Jack Bauer doesn't wear a watch. He decides what time it is.

If Jack Bauer were a burger at McDonald's, he would be called the Mc-Death.

Jack has never lost a staring match. If you attempt to enter a staring contest with Jack, it's 99% likely you will be shot within 60 seconds.

Jack Bauer uses those he has killed as tax write-offs.

Edgar Stiles had sex with seven different women last night by simply invoking Jack Bauer's name.

Jack Bauer does not need SCUBA gear. If he runs out of air, he uses anger.

Jack Bauer taught the Russians how to play Russian Roulette.

How do black boxes survive plane crashes? Because Jack Bauer holds it in his hands.

Jack Bauer has killed more people than Vin Diesel and Chuck Norris. And he does it in 24 hours.

Jack Bauer has never had to use the Backspace button on his computer.

If your power goes out, it's because Jack Bauer took it.

Jack Bauer is the only one who knows the true location of Homer Simpson's Springfield.

The Swiss Army knife MacGuyver uses was a present from Jack Bauer.

Jack Bauer is the reason the death rate in Los Angeles is so high.

Radioactive fallout won't mutate Jack Bauer. He mutates the radiation.

I once played paintball with Jack Bauer. I don't play it anymore.

Jack Bauer never has to preheat the oven.

Jack Bauer doesn't kill terrorists. They die from fear of being killed by Jack Bauer.

Jack played kickball once when he was a little boy. Now, somewhere, there is a man with "Spaulding" imprinted on his face.

Although no one can make Ashlee Simpson actually sing, Jack Bauer can make her talk.

The only way Ford will make a comeback is to come out with the Jack Bauer Explorer.

Jack Bauer once coached his daughter Kim's little league team to the championship game. To motivate the team at the beginning of the game, he was very intense and repeatedly shouted "What is your primary objective?"

The only reason CSI exists in Las Vegas is because Jack Bauer lives in Los Angeles.

Jack Bauer can ride shotgun in the driver's seat.

For most people, a red light means stop. To Jack Bauer, it means go faster.

Jack Bauer once took 25 hours to defeat a terrorist plot. This event was never aired because the entire test audience developed post traumatic stress disorder.

Nike pays royalty fees to Jack Bauer every time they use their slogan, "Just do it!"

If you click on "Who the hell is Jack Bauer," Jack Bauer will hunt you down to demonstrate what he can do.

Jack Bauer can make Minute Rice in less than a minute.

Eddie Bauer recently tried to change his company's name to Jack Bauer. His head was found in a duffel bag 2 days later.

If Jack Bauer had been the mastermind behind the robbery in Ocean's Eleven, it would have been much of a movie, because all he would have had to do would be to walk into the Bellagio and say, "My name is Jack Bauer. Give me $163 million. NOW!" End of story.

Jack Bauer can only get drunk from a combination of rattlesnake venom and hot sauce. And he's sober again in six minutes.

Jack Bauer is the only person Tony Soprano would never dream of okaying a hit on.

Jack Bauer only eats meat; he hates food that never had a pulse.

Despite Jack Bauer's protests, CTU continues to use only one safeguard against infiltration: A question on all job applications which reads, "Are you a mole?"

If Jack Bauer knows your name (and he does), just hope that he never thinks it's important. Ever.

7/11's are open 24 hours/day just in case Jack Bauer stops by for a microwaved burrito.

The CEO of American Express never leaves home without Jack Bauer.

When posed with the question, "To be, or not to be?" Jack Bauer killed Shakespeare.

When Jack Bauer lost a tooth as a child, instead of leaving a quarter, the tooth fairy left a bullet.

Jack Bauer could hijack a plane with a rubber ducky.

Jack Bauer can tie his own straightjacket.

Jack Bauer's hotmail account never expires.

Radiation needs a Jack Bauer suit.

Jack Bauer broke the first rule of Fight Club.

When the going gets tough, the tough get Jack Bauer.

Jack Bauer has a 5 o'clock shadow at 5 a.m.

The first piece of luggage to appear on the baggage carousel belongs to Jack Bauer.

Jack Bauer once played the game in which he had to guess which of three cups the ball was under. The ball promptly surrendered before he could speak.

The only thing Jack Bauer has never caught is his breath.

What happens in Jack Bauer's interrogation room stays in Jack Bauer's interrogation room.

Jack Bauer bites the bed bugs.

If you meet anyone who's an optimist, they have obviously never met Jack Bauer.

James Bond has his Bond girls. Jack Bauer has his body count.

In grade school, Jack Bauer's teachers gave him apples.

The only reason Bill Gates doesn't crush Apple is because Jack Bauer owns stock in it.

Ron Burgundy was wrong… San Diego, in fact, was named after Jack Bauer.

Jack Bauer does not need a space suit; he just holds his breath.

Jack Bauer once mistook a box of bullets for Cheerios in his cereal. He didn't notice.

Mulder and Scully left the X-Files too soon. They would've realized that the truth is Jack Bauer.

Jack Bauer is what Willis was talkin' about; he just didn't know it yet.

When Jack Bauer flushes the toilet, it goes clockwise, no matter what hemisphere he is in.

Jack Bauer did not answer questions in school. He asked them.

One day, Jack Bauer went to a Frank Sinatra concert. When Frank started to sing "My Way", Jack Bauer ran up on stage, put two rounds in Sinatra's head, and said, "No, Frank, we'll do it my way."

Jack Bauer does not drive fast; his car is just trying to get away.

Jack Bauer doesn't have to slap the bottom of the ketchup bottle to get the ketchup to come out.

Jack Bauer makes Freddy Kruger wet the bed.

Jack Bauer can birdie a par 1 hole.

Jack Bauer won the Daytona 500. On a skateboard.

Jack Bauer's the kind of guy who will swat a fly with a sledgehammer in a glass house, if he thinks the fly needs to be swatted.

Jack Bauer doesn't work in the interest of national security; the nation is interested in securing itself on Jack's good side.

Jack Bauer once beat Super Mario Brothers 3 without touching the controller. He just stared at the screen until the game beat itself.

Jack Bauer invented the Internet just so he could fight cyberterrorists.

If J.K. Rowling wrote Jack Bauer into the Harry Potter series, Voldemort would be obliterated in, like, 5 seconds.

Most people sleep with both eyes closed. Some people are believed to sleep with one eye open. As for Jack Bauer…he doesn't sleep at all. Sleep is for the weak.

If anything haunts Satan's dreams, it's Jack Bauer.

When Jack Bauer takes a shower, he never puts it back.

One of the best kept secrets of 24 is that every season of 24 happens on the summer solstice. That is why Jack always says, "Today is the longest day of my life."

Jack Bauer gives Tylenol a headache.

Hitler killed himself only after he learned that Jack Bauer was coming after him.

Jack Bauer once had to fight a tank with only a stick, a bottle cap, and four red Skittles. Jack Bauer won.

Jack Bauer gives advice to Dr. Phil.

If a company sends Jack Bauer a letter that says, "You may already have won $1,000,000", then they better give Jack a million dollars.

Satellites aren't in orbit. They're trying to get away from Jack Bauer but can't.

Jack Bauer once stared down his own image in a mirror.

Jack Bauer became the first man to successfully shoot and kill someone in each of the 50 states. 84 times.

People think Jack Bauer can't be shot because his enemies fear him, but it's really that the bullets fear Jack.

The video game God of War was originally conceptualized as Jack Bauer: the High School Years.

The reason it's so easy for terrorists to infiltrate CTU? Jack Bauer loves playing Whack-a-Mole.

If Jack Bauer were a woman, he could give birth with no anesthesia and not even wince. He may even be able to do it as a man.

If life gives you lemons, you make lemonade. If Jack Bauer gives you lemons, you'd better make him some lemonade so that you have a chance of living.

If your pizza wasn't delivered in 20 minutes or less, Jack Bauer wasn't the driver.

The original script of 24 had Jack Bauer use only his hands to kill the terrorists. Jack said give me a gun to give them a chance.

We need Jack Bauer because the US Constitution only defines Executive, Legislative, and Judicial branches of government. Apparently the framers of the constitution forgot all about the Butt-Kicking branch.

Jack Bauer makes omelets without breaking any eggs.

Edgar was attracted to Chloe only because he wanted to be closer to Jack Bauer.

When you have the remote, you're watching whatever Jack Bauer's watching.

Jack Bauer doesn't pay attention to expiration dates. He finishes all his food in 24 hours or less.

Jack Bauer scored a 2400 on the SATs. The old SATs.

Jack Bauer knows what the definition of "is" is.

Jack Bauer once punched me so hard that all of my atoms lost an electron. I'm positive.

Jack Bauer is the shortest distance between 2 points.

Jack Bauer went to Vegas and put his savings on Red 14. It stopped on double 0, but Jack still won.

Jack Bauer can eat steak with a straw.

Scariest Halloween costume in the Middle East? Well, they probably don't even celebrate Halloween. It's scary enough being a terrorist and knowing Jack Bauer is still alive.

Jack Bauer doesn't need an iPod. His ears play the song he wants to hear.

There were originally 20 hours in a day. Jack Bauer made the days longer so he could kill more terrorists in a one-day period.

Jack Bauer once popped out his eye so he could peek around a corner.

Darth Vader wears a mask because Jack Bauer is looking for the face.

Jack Bauer can blow bubbles with beef jerky.

If you killed Jack Bauer's friend and you've been shot, don't count on going to the hospital.

Nothing could get in the middle of Jack Bauer. Not even a middle name.

Jack Bauer played Bobby Fischer in chess and won by moving his rook diagonally. After Jack insisted he plays by his own rules, Bobby Fischer knocked all the pieces off the board. They are still searching for Bobby Fischer.

The film The Rock is loosely based on events from Jack Bauer's summer vacation.

When Jack Bauer attended sniper school, they changed the motto to "one shot, 100 kills."

James Bond committed suicide once he realized he had the same initials as Jack Bauer. He took the easy way out.

Jack Bauer does sleep. Sometimes when he is killing terrorists, he is actually sleepwalking.

Jack and Jill went up a hill to fetch a pail of water, but Jack Bauer thought they were fetching nukes, so he killed them both and assumed the other Jack's identity.

Jack Bauer doesn't use soft toilet paper. He doesn't use rough toilet paper. He uses sandpaper.

Jack Bauer isn't hiding from the world; the world is hiding from Jack Bauer.

Vampires dress up as Jack Bauer for Halloween.

The spoon that Neo is convinced does not exist, is daily used by Jack Bauer with his cereal.

Jack Bauer once had CTU open a socket to the depths of hell.

If Jack Bauer ever gets shot, the bullets will bleed.

Jack Bauer can open child proof medicine bottles without lining up the tabs.

If Jack Bauer worked in the Human Resources Department at CTU, there would be no moles working there.

Jack Bauer doesn't cut paper. He just angrily yells at it until it cuts itself into any shape he desires.

Jack Bauer never got picked last in kickball.

Jack Bauer could silence Simon Cowell.

Jack Bauer's clothes dry in the washing machine.

As a boy, for his birthday Jack Bauer's parents showed him how to play the game Pin the Bullet to the Head. He hasn't stopped playing it since.

Jack Bauer flosses with barbed wire.

Jack Bauer shaves with a chainsaw.

Even if you die in a violent shootout outside your bank, you're still better off than taking your chances with Jack Bauer.

The bouncer does not bother to check whether Jack Bauer is on The List.

When Darth Vader memorably uttered, "Impressive, Most Impressive", he was referring to Jack Bauer on the other side of the galaxy.

Jack Bauer kills 24 birds with one stone.

If Jack Bauer told me "I won't let anything happen to you" and then said jump off this bridge, I would do so with no fear in my mind.

The only reason why you can't see Jack Bauer on Mount Rushmore is because he doesn't want you to see him.

Jack Bauer hates microwave ovens. He finds them too slow. Jack would rather intimidate his food into going from raw to cooked in under a minute.

Jack Bauer spoke at a "Scared Straight" seminar for juvenile delinquents. All attendees requested to be transferred directly to jail at age 18.

Only Jack Bauer can prevent forest fires.

Jack Bauer flavors his food with gun powder and grated bullets.

Jack Bauer was Superman's stunt double.

Cell phone service providers need Jack Bauer to stay in business.

Jack found Waldo in one hour. The only reason he didn't find him sooner was because of daylight savings time.

Jack Bauer made hell freeze over.

If you are fortunate enough to be impregnated by Jack Bauer, be careful when the baby kicks. You are likely to be pushed across the room.

A bird in the hand is better than two in the bush. Jack Bauer never heard this saying. He ate all three birds.

Jack Bauer doesn't eat food; he interrogates it until it jumps into his mouth.

Jack Bauer doesn't clean; dust is afraid of his belongings.

Jack Bauer does not attend anger management classes but rather releases his anger by killing those who feel he should.

Jack decided to make Dirty Harry's day.

Jack Bauer and Batman have never been seen in the same place at the same time. Draw your own conclusions.

Jack Bauer has a gunshot wound, but not because he was hit. He simply wanted to feel the pain that he inflicted upon others. He was satisfied with himself.

When Jack Bauer gets within 10 miles of you, you automatically start sweating.

In space no one can hear you scream, no one except Jack Bauer.

Jack Bauer has read 3 Tom Clancy novels, two of which he re-enacted during a weekend away.

Jack Bauer has never pressed the Play button on his answering machine. When hearing beeps, he tortures the device until it gives up the messages.

When Jack Bauer wants a vacation, every terrorist in Los Angeles is dead within an hour.

Jack Bauer won in Tic-Tac-Toe in two moves.

Jack Bauer has received a grand total of $1.3 million from the tooth fairy.

Nerve gas doesn't harm Jack Bauer; it simply gets on his nerves.

The movie Under Siege would have been over in 10 minutes if it had been Jack Bauer instead of Steven Seagal. Jack would have just tipped the entire battleship over.

Jack Bauer can mix oil and water.

Jack Bauer's family crest of a picture of a barracuda eating Osama bin Laden.

Jack Bauer drinks milk after the expiration date.

The answer to the question "what happens when a strong force hits an immovable object" has never been answered because nothing that has crossed Jack Bauer's path has lived to tell about it.

Jack Bauer is never caught in traffic. That is because other vehicles fear Jack Bauer and stay out of his way.

Jack Bauer got the dark side and the light side to join him.

Jack Bauer framed Roger Rabbit.

Jack Bauer once took Kim to the zoo. When they approached the cougar cage, poor Kim screamed. Ten minutes later, the cougars were dead.

If you ever need a country annihilated, call Jack Bauer and tell him that Kim was kidnapped and killed there.

Jack Bauer won a decathlon while only competing in 9 events.

In Soviet Russia, bread stands in line for Jack Bauer.

Jack Bauer may not speak your language, but he sure as hell knows what you're saying.

There's a bullet out there with Jack Bauer's name on it. Actually, there are many of them. He has his own signature line.

When Jack Bauer needs to fly to Mexico, Mexico meets him half way.

Jack Bauer never shaves; he shoots himself in the face every morning so that his facial hair doesn't get the wrong idea.

Jack Bauer didn't save money on his car insurance by switching to Geico. The gecko is now an endangered species.

Jack Bauer controls the Matrix. He chose Neo to be the one because Jack doesn't like playing computer games.

Jack Bauer ordered Batman to name his sidekick Robin as a joke.

Jack Bauer once appeared in a Staples commercial. He broke the Easy Button because everything comes easy to Jack Bauer.

Dead men tell no tales. Except to Jack Bauer.

Jack Bauer doesn't even need to clap twice to turn the lights on.

The only true defense against Jack Bauer is a mirror.

You don't wanna say "Hello" to Jack Bauer's little friend. (*Ed's note:* A Scarface reference.)

Someone asked me how my day went, and I told them, "I feel like Jack Bauer just questioned me."

Jack Bauer doesn't interrogate. He shoots the suspect until he finds another suspect he needs information from.

The truth is out there, but only Jack Bauer knows the truth.

Jack Bauer speaks 37 languages simultaneously.

Jack Bauer paid the cougar and Kevin Dillon to keep Kim busy in Season Two. But Kim escaped because she is, of course, half Jack Bauer.

Jack Bauer wouldn't accept your friendship on Facebook.

Jack Bauer is never charged the $2 fee when using foreign ATM machines.

Jack Bauer thinks Walker Texas Ranger is a baseball team.

Jack Bauer won the four-man bobsled event at the 2006 Olympics, by himself.

A Jack Bauer interrogation has been scientifically proven more effective and accurate than the strongest truth serums known to man.

Jack Bauer doesn't wait for the bus; the bus waits for Jack Bauer.

Jack Bauer ran into an elephant, and the elephant fell down.

Jack Bauer once ate six saltine crackers in under 60 seconds, without a single sip of water.

Jack Bauer once took every drug known to man and then took a nap.

Jack Bauer can draw a perfectly straight line without a ruler.

Jack Bauer won the slam dunk contest without jumping.

Jack Bauer puts the "terror" in terrorists.

Before Jack Bauer went to Las Vegas, the slot machine was known as the "two-armed bandit".

Jack Bauer ONLY eats the crust.

Jack Bauer can win the world series of poker without being dealt a hand.

Kevin Bacon always makes sure to stay at least 7 steps away from Jack Bauer.

Jack Bauer jousted Sir Lancelot with a toothpick. And won.

Jack Bauer completes his missions in 24 hours because he hates going home with a messy desk.

Jack Bauer continually renews his magazine subscriptions on a month-to-month basis. He's running out of Time.

Jack Bauer's favorite part of school was pulling all-nighters.

Jack Bauer was the only person that voted for Palmer.

Jack Bauer once fell into quicksand. Lucky for Jack, he had his gun and shot his way out of it.

The little light in Jack Bauer's refrigerator stays on even after the door is closed.

Jack Bauer does not wash his clothes. Jack Bauer's clothes stay clean for fear of reprisals.

CONPLAN 8888: COUNTER-ZOMBIE DOMINANCE

One source of metaphors for the behaviors of the numerous threats to the US around the world has been the fascination with zombies in the 2010s. Spurred on by *Zombieland, Dawn of the Dead, World War Z, The Walking Dead*, and other sources, zombie culture's strict codes of ethics—aggressiveness, ruthlessness, determination, focus, and goal-setting—have served as stand-ins for many potential targets, be they terrorists, rogue nations, narcos, cyber attackers, proliferators, or insurgents.

One of the IC's most popular discussion groups has been devoted to the parallels between zombie behavior and this litany of intelligence topics. The descriptors used for zombies are often those we use for our enemies: incapable of error (the 10-foot tall rational actor model); never admitting to having made an error, unwilling to negotiate, monolithic in motivation.

This fascination is best seen in the following outtakes of the Pentagon's ConPlan 8888, written in the style of more standard ConPlans. It can be interpreted in part as a way of teaching the DOD style of writing. I've changed some of the formatting, typos, and usage for ease of reading and so as not to reveal potentially sensitive information on how such plans would look to the cognoscenti.

CONPLAN 8888

Headquarters United States Strategic Command

CDRUSSTRATCOM CONPLAN 8888-11

"Counter-Zombie Dominance"

30 Apr 2011

Classified by: N/A
Reason: N/A
Declassify on: N/A

CONTENTS (as specified below)

DISCLAIMER

Conplan 8888 Disclaimer: This plan was not actually designed as a joke. During the summers of 2009 and 2010, while training augmentees from a local training squadron about the JOPP (Joint Operation Planning Process), members of a USSTRATCOM (Strategic Command) component found out (by accident) that the hyperbole involved in writing a "zombie survival plan" actually provided a very useful and effective training tool. Planners who attended JPME II (Joint Professional Military Education) at the Joint Combined Warfighting School (JCWS) also realized that training examples for plans must accommodate the political fallout that occurs if the general public mistakenly believes that a fictional training scenario is actually a real plan. Rather than risk such an outcome by teaching our augmentees using the fictional "Tunisia" or "Nigeria" scenarios used at JCWS, we elected to use a completely-impossible scenario that could never be mistaken as a real plan.

Because the plan was so ridiculous, our students not only enjoyed the lessons; they actually were able to explore the basic concepts of plan and order development (fact, assumptions, specified and implied tasks, references, etc.) very effectively.

We posted this plan because we feel it is a very enjoyable way to train new planners and boost retention of critical knowledge. We posted this after reading about the benefits of crowd sourcing phenomena in the business management book *The Starfish and the Spider.* Our intent was to place this training tool "in the wild" so that others who were interested in finding new and innovative way to train planners could have an alternative and admittedly unconventional tool at their disposal that could be modified and updated over time. We also hoped that this type of non-traditional training approach would provide inspiration for other personnel trying to teach topics that can be very boring. Finally we figured that an entry like this would not only be instructive, but possibly entertaining for personnel deployed away from their families supporting military ops abroad. If this plan helps illustrate how JOPP works and brings a smile or a brief laugh in the process, so much the better.

If you suspend reality for a few minutes, this type of training scenario can actually take a very dry, monotonous topic and turn it into something rather enjoyable. (*Ed's Note:* CIA's Office of Security has used similarly creative methods to teach computer security, borrowing from such shows as *24, The Office, Blair Witch Project, Mythbusters,* and other popular movies and television series in crafting more approachable computer-based learning to topics they deemed otherwise boring.)

SECURITY INSTRUCTIONS

1. The long title of this plan is CFDRUSSTRATCOM CONPLAN 8888-11 Counter-Zombie Dominance Operations.
2. The short tile of this plan is CFDRUSSTRATCOM CONPLAN 8888-11.
3. This document is UNCLASSIFIED to ensure maximum utility during times of crisis. Classified capabilities used to counter zombies will be addressed in appropriate orders and annexes adapted during crisis action planning to adapt the actions in this plan to current operational conditions.
4. This document contains information affecting the national defense of the United States within the meaning of the Espionage Laws, title 18, United States Code, sections 379 and 794. The transmission or revelation of information contained herein, in any manner, to an unauthorized person is prohibited by law.

PURPOSE

This plan fulfills fictional Contingency Planning Guidance (CPG) tasking for USTRATCOM to develop a comprehensive JOPES (Joint Planning and Execution System) Level 3 plan to undertake military operations to preserve "non-zombie" humans from the threats posed by a zombie horde. Because zombies pose a threat to all "non-zombie" human life (hereafter referred to as "humans"), USSTRATCOM will be prepared to preserve the sanctity of human life and conduct operations in support of any human population—including traditional adversaries. The objective of this plan is threefold:

- Establish and maintain a vigilant defensive condition aimed at protecting humankind from zombies.
- If necessary, conduct operations that will, if directed, eradicate zombie threats to human safety.
- Aid civil authorities in maintaining law and order and restoring basic services during and after a zombie attack.

DEFENSIVE OPERATIONS

Those operations aimed at monitoring the environment for zombie-related threats and preparing capabilities to respond to the same. This plan's defensive branch (within Annex C) details protective and preventive measures for humans in response to the threat scenarios identified in Paragraph 6 below. The system of Zombie Conditions (Z-CONS or ZOMBIECONS) will provide predetermined actions to proactively position the USSTRATCOM enterprise in response to threat indications and warning.

OFFENSIVE OPERATIONS

Those operations where USSTRATCOM has been directed to eradicate zombie threats to human safety using military capabilities as authorized by POTUS and SECDEF. This plan's "offensive" branch (within Annex C and Annex S (STO)) details the neutralization (to ender ineffective) of zombie capabilities through denial, deception, disruption, degradation or destruction. The system of ZOMBIECONS will proactively anticipate and respond to increased GCC space capability requirements including offensive space control capabilities.

CONDITIONS FOR IMPLEMENTATION

Politico-Military Situation. Zombies are horribly dangerous to all human life and zombie infections have the potential to seriously undermine national security and economic activities that sustain our way of life. Therefore, having a population that is not composed of zombies or at risk from their malign influence is vital to US and Allied national interests. While the US currently enjoys several asymmetric advantages against zombie infections originating in the Eurasian landmass, these advantages can easily be negated by air and sea traffic that could transport the source of a zombie infection to North and South America. Further, asteroids and nuclear space radiation that can convert people into zombies can affect any landmass or population on earth. Given the rapidity at which zombie outbreaks spread, decisive, overwhelming, and possibly unilateral military force may be required to negate the zombie threat.

PLAN EXECUTION

CONPLAN 8888 is designed to be implemented across all 6 phases of military operations. When directed by POTUS or SECDEF, DCRUSSTRATCOM will issue mission type orders (ALTERORD, WARNORD, DEPORD, OPORD, EXORD, TERMORD) to execute specific actions from this plan. This plan is only designed to be implemented if zombie threats arise which cannot be handled within the scope of the USSTRATCOM Campaign Plan (OPLAN 8000) and the current Fiscal Year OPORDS (FY XX OPORD, SPACE OPORD, DSCA OPORD, etc.) that direct the execution of actions from OPLAN 8000.

ZOMBIE THREAT SUMMARY

CONPLAN 8888 is designed to address the following types of zombie threats:

Pathogenic Zombies: PZs are zombie life forms created after an organism is infected by a virus or bacteria or some other form of contagion.

Radiation Zombies: RZs are zombie life forms created after an organism is infected by an extreme dosage of electromagnetic and/or particle radiation.

Evil Magic Zombies: EMZs are zombie life forms created by some form of occult experimentation in what might otherwise be referred to as "evil magic".

Space Zombies: SZs are zombie life forms originating from space or created by toxic contamination of the earth environment via some form of extra-terrestrial toxin or radiation.

"Zombie satellites" can be classified as SZs, however, they pose no danger to humans (unless they conduct an unplanned de-orbit). Typically, zombie satellites only pose a threat o the SATCOM services like DirectTV (refer to Galaxy 15 incident-May 2010)

Weaponized Zombies: WZs are zombie life forms deliberately created via bio/bio-mechanical engineering for the purpose of being employed as weapons. Zombie weaponization programs and supporting infrastructures are included in COAs to deal with these threats. The movie *The Crazies* exemplifies the most common type of WZ (humans turned into zombies via exposure to toxic chemicals/gasses).

Symbiant-Induced Zombies: SIZs are zombie life forms originating from the introduction of a symbiant life form into an otherwise healthy host. Although the symptoms of symbiant zombieism are similar in most regards to pathogenic zombieism, the symbiant does not kill the host organism quickly, or at all. However, there is no known way to save an organism after zombieism has occurred—even if the symbiant is removed.

Vegetarian Zombies: VZs are zombie life forms originating from any cause but pose no direct threat to humans because they only eat plant life (as indicated in the popular game *Plants Vs. Zombies*). Although VZs do not attack humans or other animal life, they will consume all plant life in front of them. They can cause massive de-forestation or elimination of basic food crops essential to humans (rice, corn, soybeans). Of note, where normal carnivorous zombies commonly groan the word "brains" semi-comprehensibly, VZs can be identified by their aversion to humans, affinity for plants and their tendency to semi-comprehensibly groan the word "grains".

Chicken Zombies: Although this sounds ridiculous, this is actually the only proven class of zombie that actually exists. CZs were first documented in Jonathan M. Forrester's 4 Dec 2006 online article "Zombie Chickens Taking Over California". CZs occur when old hens that can no longer lay eggs are incorrectly euthanized by poultry farmers using carbon monoxide. The hens are then deposited in large piles to decompose. The hens appear to be dead when buried, but inexplicably come back to life and dig themselves out from the piles of dead chickens. After reaching the surface, CZs stagger about for a period of time before ultimately expiring due to internal organ failure. CZs are simply terrifying to behold and are likely only to make people become vegetarians in protest to animal cruelty. They appear to be no direct threat to humans. They are different from WZs because they are the result of actions taken to kill a living organism vice actions taken to deliberately re-animate dead organisms or impair life functions to a minimal function.

ENVIRONMENTAL EFFECTS

Causes of zombie infection are generally resistant to most environment effects. The following environmental factors apply to zombies in this plan:

The viral pathogens that cause PZs have some vulnerability to ultraviolet light. UV light impairs the functions of ribonucleic acids (RNA) that comprise most viral life forms. At best, UV light can disrupt virus reproduction in healthy cells. It should be noted that PZs may experience painful photosensitivity as a result of sunlight exposure. For this reason, PZ activity is not expected to be as high during bright sunny conditions as it is during the hours of darkness.

EMZ, SZ, VZ, and WZs are all likely immune to any extreme meteorological phenomena except fires, floods, tornados, or tsunamis.

The following environmental factors apply to humans in this plan:

Rain will be vitally important to human survival. If civil water supplies are cut off, humans will have to rely on other means to obtain water.

Ground water from streams and rivers will be unreliable since it will be difficult to determine if ground water is a vector for zombie infection.

Humans who do not shelter-in-place within a sturdy structure that protects them from the direct effects of air currents that could carry pathogens or toxins or direct exposure to radiation will be at increased risk of contamination, death and injury.

Although these threat scenarios aren't meant to be all-inclusive (USSTRATCOM must be postured and flexible enough to respond to any emerging threat due to different zombie disaster scenarios.) Annex C Appendix 1 – Defensive Operations and Annex C Appendix 2 – Offensive Operations provide a solid foundation for full spectrum operations against most postulated zombie threats.

LEGAL CONSIDERATIONS

US and international law regulate military operations only insofar as human and animal life are concerned. There are almost no restrictions on hostile actions that may be taken either defensively or offensively against pathogenic life forms, organic-robotic entities, or "traditional" zombies. Given the likelihood of an all-out threat to "human survival", it is likely that this plan will be executed concurrently with a declaration of martial law within CONUS and US territories. Additional legal considerations taken into account when preparing this plan include: applicable US statutes, the UN Charter, international treaties and agreements to which the US is a party, the Law of Armed Conflict (LOAC), customary international law, and applicable Rules of Engagement (ROE) and policies.

OPERATIONS TO BE CONDUCTED:

Deployment: USSTRATCOM forces specified in the "forces" table of the current fiscal year OPORD are deployed around the globe. This CONPLAN has no pre-identified primary adversaries; therefore, it does not direct forward deployment of forces into a particular region. When USSTRATCOM is the "supported" CCDR, USSTRATCOM will develop during crisis, a Time-Phased Force and Deployment Data (TPFDD) in collaboration with USTRANSCOM, for those situations when offensive or defensive operations require movement of forces or assets. However, when USSTRATCOM deploys forces as a "supporting" commander, those forces will normally be tied to the "supported" theater commander's TPFDD.

Employment: CONPLAN 8888 is situationally dependent. It is designed to allow CDRUSSTRATCOM execute military operations in support of national OR theater objectives in either a supporting OR supported role. Operational phases within this plan may be sequential, non-sequential, or modified based on the global situation. However, given the global threat to humanity posed by zombies, once CDRUSSTRATCOM issues orders to transition to a specific phase of operations, that phase will apply to the entire global.

CONPLAN PHASES

Phase 0—Shape the Environment (Day-to-Day Operations). USSTRATCOM will perform routine operations to include epidemiological surveillance to watch for changes in disease vectors that could cause zombieism. USSTRATCOM Center for Combating Weapons of Mass Destruction (SCC-WMD) will serve as the lead component within the command to ensure all Phase 0 shaping operations are conducted and synchronized with other federal, state and tribal agencies. SCC-WMD will ensure that necessary epidemiological ISR requirements are issued and answered by the Intelligence Community. SCC-WMD will work with USAMRIID to ensure the risks to USSTRATCOM forces are monitored and that necessary HAZMAT and CBRNE training is accomplished across the USSTRATCOM enterprise.

Phase 1—Deter (Day-to-Day Operations). Upon receipt of a CDRUSSTRATCOM WARNORD, JFCC GS will become the supported commander for Phase 1 operations in this plan. It is important to note that zombies are not cognizant life-forms. As such, they cannot be deterred from further action. These forces include but are not limited to nation states and terrorist groups with WMD programs, unethical bio-research companies. To meet deterrence goals, USSTRATCOM will conduct large-scale training to demonstrate USSTRATCOM ability to survive and operate in a toxic/contaminated environment IOT deter nation states from pursuing development or deployment of zombie-creating pathogens, toxins or similar capabilities developed by nation states, large corporations, or terrorist/criminal groups.

Phase 2—Seize the Initiative (Evaluate/Mitigate/Prepare). Upon receipt of a CDRUSSTRATCOM WARNORD or ALERTORD, all components will initiate a force-wide recall of all assigned personnel and activate COOP Plans. All airborne and ground-based survivable C2 nodes will make ready to deploy for at least 35 days. To avoid ambiguity with nuclear-armed peers such as Russia and the PRC, USSTRATCOM will conduct confidence-building measures to ensure leaders within these nations do not construe USSTRATCOM preparations to counter zombie-dominance as preparations for war. If necessary, JFCC GS will sortie forces to conduct prompt global strikes against initial concentrations of zombies. Other USSTRATCOM forces will provide security assistance to federal, state and tribal authorities to negate zombie threats, provide ISR and security for protected civilian areas and will aid in the enforcement of quarantine zones.

Phase 3—Dominate (Respond/Counter). Upon receipt of a CDRUSSTRATCOM order (ALERTORD, WARNORD, OPORD, EXORD), all USSTRATCOM forces will begin preparations to conduct combat operations against zombie threats. USSTRATCOM strategic task forces (Task Forces (TF) 124, 134, 144, 204, 214, 294, and/or other TFs formed to support strategic ops) will make combat preparations IAW applicable EAT-STRAT volumes. USSTRATCOM forces will activate COOP plans, emergency disaster support plans and will shelter all mission essential personnel in place for at least 40 days.

Phase 4/5—Stabilize Environment. No earlier than 40 days after the initiation of Phase 3 operations, USSTRATCOM forces will initiate local reconnaissance ops to determine the severity of the remaining zombie threat, assess the physical and epidemiological security of the local environment, and survey the status of basic services (water, power, sewage infrastructure and water, air, land lines of communications). All reports back to HQ USSTRATCOM will be broadcast in clear text using unsecured comms so that if any isolated survivors intercept those comms, link-up between these survivors and USSTRATCOM forces will be facilitated. USSTRATCOM forces will remain "combat ready" to re-engage any remaining pockets of zombie forces or contamination vectors.

Enable Civil Authority (Normalization). USSTRATCOM, its components, other applicable CCDRs, and industry partners will collaboratively replace, recover, rebuild, and reconstitute, US/civil/commercial/Allied civil infrastructure and services, as needed. USSTRATCOM will continue to provide support to theater warfighters and USG agencies, as required. Lessons Learned and After Action Reports IAW (see Enclosure D to CJCSI 3150.25B) will be produced and fed back into this CONPLAN for process improvement and inclusion in future exercises.

SUPPORTING PLANS

Supporting Plans. Due to the fact that an outbreak of zombieism will likely spread rapid across COCOM AOR boundaries, CDRUSSTRATCOM has been tasked by SECDEF to develop a Level 3 plan that can serve as the model for all other COCOM counter-zombie dominance planning. CONPLAN 8888 planning guidance from the SECDEF assumes a worst-case scenario in which all normal C2 capabilities are impaired or overrun by zombie forces. As such, this plan relies heavily on hardened C2 capabilities normally reserved for nuclear or full scale global conventional warfare. Supporting Combatant Commands, and functional components will update their contingency plans related to counter-zombie operations using this plan.

COLLATERAL PLANS

Collateral Plans. The following USSTRATCOM plans may be implemented collaterally with CONPLAN 8888.

CDRUSSTRATCOM

CONPLAN 8035 "Space Operations"

CONPLAN 8531 "Pandemic Influenza"

CONPLAN 8099 "Combating Weapons of Mass Destruction"

OPLAN 8010 "Deterrence and Global Strike"

OPLAN 8001 "Omnibus Support Plan"

Geographic Combatant Command OPLANS or CONPLANs:

Refer to OPLAN 8001 "Omnibus Support Plan"

ASSUMPTIONS

a. US and Allies will have the situational awareness necessary to conduct all counter-zombie dominance operations in this plan.

b. Zombie forces will become stronger with each human casualty (because each human casualty will become a zombie).

c. US and Allied forces may be degraded as a conflict emerges and progresses.

d. LOAC will not apply to zombies.

e. Domestic law enforcement agencies will address any CONUS-based attacks involving zombies until martial law is declared.

f. There is no medical cure for zombieism. Once a human turns into a zombie, they cannot be cured or reverted to human status.

g. The only way to ensure a zombie is "dead" is to burn the zombie corpse. EMZs are the only class of zombie that may not be vulnerable to this measure.

h. The Chaplain Corps may provide the only viable means of combating EMZs. As such, atheists could be particularly vulnerable to EMZ threats.

i. Because accurate intelligence related to zombies will be hard to obtain suing traditional methods, planners will have to assume worst-case scenarios derived from popular culture references (books, movies, comic books) to adequately model zombie threats.

j. Even if infected by zombie contaminant or pathogen, human biology requires a regular intake of water and food. Absent proper hydration to offset the effects of progressing zombieism, zombie-infected humans will experience organ failure that will immobilize or kill the host within 30-40 days.

k. Marketing materials for most hand sanitizer products indicate the product kills 99% of all germs. Although none of these products has ever indicated any efficacy against biohazard level 4 pathogens like ebola, it is entirely possible that such products could limit or delay the spread of pathogen-based zombieism if properly employed.

OPERATIONAL LIMITATIONS

Operational Limitations consist of actions or conditions that USSTRATCOM and its supporting forces must take or ensure happen (constraints) and those actions or conditions that USSTRATCOM and its supporting forces must not take or allow to happen (restraint). Other limitations contained in this section pertain to resource or procedural shortfalls that planners must consider which could undermine USSTRATCOM's ability to achieve the missions outlined in this plan.

CONSTRAINTS

USSTRATCOM forces must:

a. Remain postured to deter adversaries from attacking the US or its allies with WMD.

b. Continue to conduct assigned missions throughout all phases of a zombie apocalypse.

c. Remain postured to conduct military operations to repel zombies and eradicate their safe havens.

d. Be prepared to conduct combat operations within CONUS against zombie populations that were previously US citizens.

e. Maintain viable, up-to-date continuity of operations plans.

f. Maintain emergency plans to employ nuclear weapons within CONUS to eradicate zombie hordes.

RESTRAINTS

USSTRATCOM forces must not:

a. Allow nuclear weapon storage areas to be compromised by zombie forces.

b. Allow airfields or POL facilities critical to combat aircraft capabilities to be overrun by zombie forces.

c. Allow maritime facilities that support SSBN operations to be compromised by zombie forces.

SHORTFALLS AND LIMITING FACTORS

a. Adequate zombie defenses require sandbags, sand, barbed wire, anti-personnel mines, riot control chemical agents, MOPP-gear and petroleum (to create flame barriers). These supplies may not be present in sufficient volume to allow desired levels of defense against zombie incursion and could severely tax available logistical support infrastructure.

b. USSTRATCOM forces do not currently hold enough contingency stores (food, water) to support 30 days of barricaded counter-zombie operations.

c. USSTRATCOM has no ground combat forces capable of repelling a zombie assault.

d. USSTRATCOM can only deliver synchronized fires against a zombie threat via strategic air, space and maritime forces.

e. USSTRATCOM Offutt AFB provides the only semi-hardened location capable of sheltering personnel responsible for commanding and controlling a coordinated combat action against zombie forces. JFCC SPACE and USCYBERCOM operations centers are located within protected military facilities. However, zombie forces will likely overrun those installations within the first days of a zombie invasion.

f. USSTRATCOM Component-level continuity of operations plans (COOP) do not currently address zombie threats. Further, since component COOP(s) utilize facilities provided by other USSTRATCOM components or non-hardened temporary facilities, zombie threats will likely render COOP(s) ineffective. COOP(s) should be revised to include in-extremis carpentry, welding, and lumber stockpiling and training in metal work in order to facilitate shelter-in-place ops and barricading of unhardened facilities against zombies.

g. Airborne Command Centers are unlikely to be viable after the first week of a zombie invasion. Although refueling in air will extend mission capabilities, the support bases that refuelers operate from will likely be overrun by zombies. It is possible that islands like Hawaii, Guam and Diego Garcia might remain viable relocation bases if airborne C2 assets can make it to these locations.

h. Time To Commence Effective Operations. Because of the unique situation surrounding zombie threats and the level of USG interests at stake, it is unlikely there will be a time-phased, incremental buildup of forces. It is more likely that during COA development, USSTRATCOM will coordinate joint and combined military efforts, options, levels of forces and objectives with other affected COCOMs, based on worldwide situational awareness and guidance from OSD, Joint Staff, and other combatant commands.

COMMAND RELATIONSHIPS

(See 8888 Annex J and current operational orders.)

Command Relationships. USSTRATCOM forces may be fixed or deployed, and may support theater and/or national objectives simultaneously. USSTRATCOM exercises COCOM over assigned forces and utilizes support relationships to support other commands. USSTRATCOM will tailor command relations to best match the situation, taking into account the global perspective and other ongoing space missions. Therefore, there is no "one size fits all" for counter-zombie operations command relationships.

CDRUSSTRATCOM has COCOM of all forces as assigned in the Forces for Unified Commands section of the SECDEF's Global Force management Implementation Guidance. Commanders of USSTRATCOM Sub-Unified Commands and Components normally retain OPCON of fixed and deployed forces. These command relationships will be utilized during counter-zombie operations unless otherwise directed by SECDEF.

LOGISTICS APPRAISAL

Logistics Appraisal. Forces utilized in this CONPLAN include deployable or fixed assets operating in CONUS or from sites located throughout the world and are controlled as separate forces. During a contingency, USSTRATCOM service components will ensure all mission-critical forces (fixed and mobile), are fully supported and capable of performing their mission. Forces fixed in another COCOM AOR are authorized DIRLAUTH with the COCOMs responsible for their AORs for the purpose of coordinating their support requirements. These forces will keep USSTRATCOM and their owning component informed. COCOMs will work with USSTRATCOM J4 and J8 for reimbursement for support requested by USSTRATCOM forces (See Annex D).

CLASSIFICATION GUIDANCE

This classification guidance provides users with general categories of subjects and levels of protection. The level of protection listed represents the highest probable level of protection required by these subjects during specific plan phases. If a document derived from this plan contains particular portions that are unclassified when standing alone, but classified information will be revealed when they are combined or associated, those portions shall be marked as unclassified and the page shall be marked with the highest classification of any information on or revealed by the page. An explanation will be added to the page or document identifying the combination or association of information that necessitated the higher classification. (*Ed's note:* Chart deleted by editor.)

Changes to this guidance will be coordinated through USSTRATCOM J53.

Agencies identified in Annex Z may reproduce this plan consistent with need-to-know. Listed organizations may reproduce and distribute this plan to assigned forces as required to fulfill mission requirements, and as required for preparation of supporting plans.

Non-DoD agencies with a need to know will be allowed to make copies of this plan or hand scribe significant portions of the plan if necessary.

Release to US, Australian, Canadian and United Kingdom personnel with a valid need-to-know is authorized. Contact USSTRATCOM/J53 to obtain permission to release or disclose this plan to other foreign personnel.

BASIC PLAN (ANNEX A)

References

The Zombie Survival Guide: Complete Protection from the Living Dead, by Max Brooks (Three Rivers Press), 16 Sep 2003.

The Zombie Survival Guide: Recorded Attacks, by Max Brooks (Three Rivers Press), 6 Oct 2009.

World War Z: An Oral History of the Zombie War, by Max Brooks (Three Rivers Press), 16 Oct 2007

The Zombie Combat Manual: A Guide to Fighting the Living Dead (Berkley Trade) 6 April 2010

"Zombie Chickens Taking Over California" Jonathan M. Forrester, 4 Dec 06 (http://www.slashfood.com/2006/12/04/Zombie-Chickens-Taking-Over-California/)

Zombies Vs. Unicorns, by Justine Larbastier and Holly Black (Margaret K. McElderry Books, NYC), 2010.

SITUATION

a. General. Although there is no specific Contingency Planning Guidance (CPG) within the Chairman's Guidance for Employment of the Force (GEF) directing the creation of a counter-zombie dominance plan, there is ample specified guidance for the creation of Level-3 plans to provide Defense Support to Civil Authorities (DSCA), Homeland Defense (HD), Counter-Weapons of Mass Destruction (CWMD), and Pandemic Influenza (PI).

b. In light of the inherent survival threat posed by zombies and absent specified guidance for detailed planning to address such a contingency, USSTRATCOM has taken the initiative to develop a JOPES Level

3 plan (CONPLAN) consistent with guidance derived from other specified planning efforts to ensure US and Allied freedom of action from zombie domination. As a result, many specified tasks documented in this plan are taken from high-level strategic guidance documents. Other tasks in the plans derived from these higher level tasks or essential for their accomplishments are listed as "implied tasks". In all cases, CDRUSSTRATCOM has determined which tasks are "essential" tasks based on mission analysis (unless higher level guidance already specified that a task is essential).

c. Science provides almost no useful data about zombies. Although this presents a number of challenges when military planners design operations to counter zombies, this plan utilizes data provided by science fiction sources in addition to what little academic/scientific information is currently available. The use of science fiction sources does provide a compelling advantage for military planners, however. In almost all cases, science fiction scenarios significantly enhance analyses of courses of actions, facilitate COA wargaming and adjustment, and provide insight for planners with regards to the development of facts, assumptions, risks and aversion of "groupthink" or "cognitive bias". In short, the more roust a science fiction scenario related to zombies is, the more useful it is for planning purposes, regardless of how "outlandish" it might be.

EXECUTION

Execution of this plan requires a USSTRATCOM EXORD. Activation or preparation to carry out operations detailed within this plan (including but not limited to changing phases, changing Zombie-Cons, or terminating operations) will require an USSTRATCOM ALERTORD at a minimum.

MISSION STATEMENT

On order, CDRUSSTRATCOM will execute global military operations to protect humankind from zombies and, if directed, eradicate zombie threats to human safety and aid civil authorities in maintaining law and order and restoring basic services during and after a zombie attack.

COMMANDER'S INTENT

Purpose: CDRUSSTRATCOM will conduct military operations unilaterally or in conjunction with Allies to preserve the collective security of humankind.

Method: CDRUSSTRATCOM will utilize assigned and attached military forces to maintain timely and accurate warning of zombie threats, target zombie safe havens, eliminate sources of zombieism, and provide aid to civil authorities in their efforts to protect civilians from zombie threats.

End State: Sources of zombieism are eradicated, zombie forces are precluded from massing and threatening human population centers and potential adversaries are deterred from developing zombie weaponization programs.

AREAS OF CONCERN

Area of Responsibility (AOR). CDRUSSTRATCOM, as a combatant commander, is not assigned an AOR for normal operations and will not exercise those functions of command associated with a geographic AOR. Although CDRUSSTRATCOM has no geographic AOR and has no specified combat roles against zombies, he is the only CCDR in control of nuclear weapons—which are likely to be the most effective weapons against hordes of the undead. CDRUSSTRATCOM serves as the single point of contact for all global deterrence, global strike, military space, and cyber operations as directed by the President of the United States (POTUS) or Secretary of Defense (SECDEF) for the protection of US government (USG), and those civilian, commercial and Allied capabilities augmenting the USG.

Area of Interest (AOI). Any terrestrial, atmospheric or exo-atmospheric location where a source of zombieism or massed zombie forces are currently positioned.

Joint Operational Area (JOA). Although USSTRATCOM has global responsibilities and no geographic AOR, orders utilized to activate any portion of this plan will designate JOAs to aid in the prioritization and synchronization of efforts. For the purposes of this plan, JOAs will not cross Geographic COCOM AOR boundaries as defined in the UCP. If threats exist in areas adjacent to COCOM AOR boundaries, then two or more JOAs will be designated and the geographic COCOM supporting USSTRATCOM whose AOR contains a JOA for counter-zombie ops will be responsible for that operational area IAQ USSTRATCOM or SECDEF orders.

FLEXIBLE DETERRENT OPTIONS

Flexible Deterrent Options (FDOs): Applicable only for nation states or evil magicians who are capable of creating Weaponized Zombies (WZ) or Evil Magic Zombies (EMZ). Refer to Annex C for additional details and Counter-Zombie Dominance Flexible Deterrent Option.

Zombies cannot be deterred.

ENEMY FORCES

There are eight classes of Zombies addressed within this plan. Chicken Zombies pose no threat to humans and actions to counter CZs are the responsibilities of the US Depts of Justice, Homeland Security, Agriculture, and Food and Drug Administration. The Zombie threat classes are: Pathogenic Zombies (PZ); Radiation Zombies (RZ): Evil Magic Zombies (EMZ); Space Zombies (SZ); Weaponized Zombies (WZ): Symbiant-Induced Zombies (SIZ); Vegetarian Zombies (VZ).

Of the eight classes of zombies, four are caused by "natural" phenomena that can be reliably monitored and predicted.Zombies caused by natural phenomena are: PZ, RZ, SZ, and SIZ.

RZ can also be caused by man-made phenomena.

Of the eight classes of zombies, two are caused by "man-made" or "engineered" phenomena that can be reliably monitored and predicted. Zombies caused by man-made phenomena are: RZ and WZ.

RZ can also be caused by natural phenomena.

Of the eight classes of zombies, one type of caused by "occult" phenomena that cannot be reliably monitored, predicted, or proven to exist. Zombies caused by occult phenomena are: EMZ.

Based on most science fiction sources, EMZ, despite being the hardest threats to eliminate directly (by attacking the zombie life form) can usually be eliminated if the source of evil magic is destroyed. There is evidence to suggest the Chaplain Corps may prove integral to countering these threats.

Of the eight classes of zombies, one type of created by undetermined phenomena. Zombies caused by natural phenomena are: VZ.

This class of zombie has been document in the popular video game "Plants Vs. Zombies" and the movie "Signs" starring the actor Mel Gibson. No current examples of this zombie class have ever been captured or examined by scientists.

Planning. For planning purposes, the worst case threat scenario for this CONPLAN is the emergency of a zombie phenomena of high transmissibility, high attack rates, high virulence, little or no immunity, and limited effective countermeasures (only susceptible to destruction of the brain stem). This event would produce a situation in which DoD would experience significant negative impacts on readiness (e.g., personnel availability, training, unit manning, equipping and deploying the force) while being simultaneously directed to provide substantial support to civil authorities and deter and/or respond to opportunistic adversarial aggression.

The primary characteristics of a highly threatening zombie phenomenon are the pathogen's ability to invade a host without being observed (bite or other visible wounds *not* being required), the ability to successfully reproduce within a host (human, animal or plant), its ability to exploit abundant natural hosts or vectors (not just limited to humans but able to spread among a host of animals or even plants), a potential to mutate quickly (mitigating our ability to develop a vaccine or "cure"), and high transmissibility resulting in large numbers of people becoming sick or absent simultaneously (or entire herds, flocks or crops being infected or contaminated).

A second order effect of a zombie phenomenon of operational significance is the potential for political, social, and/or economic instability and/or degradation of allied military readiness. While adversarial forces (or resources) may also be infected, their readiness, operational capability or domestic stability may not be impacted in the same manner, to the same degree, or at the same time as US and allied forces. The degree to which countries and regions can mitigate morbidity, mortality and associated effects during the zombie phenomena event and reintegrate recovering (if possible) individuals and agricultural systems into society will have a considerable impact on military force capabilities. Countries with more advanced, prepared and robust health care and agricultural systems (to include a responsive quarantine capability) will be better able to mitigate many of the zombie phenomenon effects.

Key security concerns that would arise from a zombie phenomenon event of operational significance include opportunistic aggression, opportunities for violent extremists to acquire Weapons of Mass Destruction (WMD) during reduced security capabilities, reduced partner capacity during and after a zombie phenomenon, instability resulting from a humanitarian disaster, and decreased production and distribution of essential commodities. The prevalence of a zombie phenomenon coupled with political, social and economic instability may result in reduced security capabilities, providing an opportunity for international military conflict, increased terrorist activity, internal unrest, political and/or economic collapse, humanitarian crises, and dramatic civil unrest.

Enemy Center of Gravity (COG). Once a zombie phenomenon is capable of efficient, effective, and sustained transmission, its COG will be the geographic speed at which it can spread, attack rate within the host population, and the virulence of the zombie phenomenon. A zombie phenomenon will produce cascading effects due to the large number of simultaneous absences over extended periods of time or loss of significant critical infrastructure/key resources (e.g., agricultural resources) on a national, regional or international scale.

Critical Capabilities. The ability to efficiently and effectively reproduce within a host, mutate quickly, and effectively transmit from host to host are key requisites for the realization of a worst-case zombie phenomenon scenario. The degree of transmissibility depends on a number of key factors such as pathogen mutation, transmissibility of a new strain among hosts or vectors, proximity and behavior of hosts or vectors (e.g., travel between population centers or processing facilities), survivability outside a host) e.g., ability to spread via fomites) and availability/effectiveness of countermeasures.

Critical Requirements. A critical requirement of the zombie phenomenon is the ability to mutate and propagate among and between hosts. Efficient transmission can occur in a number of ways, including respiratory/airborne spread, direct contact, food and water contamination, biological vectors (e.g., mosquitoes, sand flies, ticks), and via fomites (e.g., doorknobs, desktops, vehicles, machinery) where the disease can potentially survive for hours or days. Additionally, disease impacts severe enough to incapacitate or render unusable large numbers of hosts will likely generate additional psychological impacts among a population (absenteeism due to fear and panic, hoarding, trade restrictions). Furthermore, the infected host must survive long enough to shed disease agent in sufficient quantity to infect others. Because zombies do not expire naturally as is the case with humans suffering from other diseases (such as influenza or ebola), there is no inherent brake on the spread of the disease. Finally, the disease requires susceptible populations, which includes those that are immunologically naïve and inadequately trained on preventive, environmental or occupational health measures. (Note: The spread of the zombie effect via either respiratory/airborne means or through fomites is considered the most highly dangerous course of action and the least likely based on historical evidence.)

Critical Vulnerabilities. The disease agent cannot infect an immunologically protected host (should such a capability be developed) and is susceptible to non-pharmaceutical intervention measures, various forms of environmental disinfection, vector control, development of effective immune response by vaccine or natural infection, and pharmaceutical prophylaxis or treatment. Non-pharmaceutical interventions include targeted, layered containment (social distancing, use of Personal Protective Equipment (PPE), non-exposure, hand-washing, disinfection, isolation/quarantine, culling, equipment sanitation, etc.) which can impede transmission.

FRIENDLY FORCES

(Refer to References C and E for detailed listing)

DECISIVE POINTS/CENTERS OF GRAVITY (COGs)

COG: Zombie forces can be expected to center their efforts against the following Centers of Gravity.

Strategic COG #1: Human population centers.

All Zombie classes will target human population centers or create effects against human population centers that will undermine human safety, security and the delivery of basic services. VZs will target agriculture resources that humans depend on.

Operational COG #1: Lines of Communication (LOC)

Zombies cannot drive, climb or swim (although zombies can wade into water, they cannot float or swim). Zombies will utilize surface roads to reach human population centers and to increase their numbers by attacking fleeing humans. Although waterways are likely to remain viable, humans can only use them safely if they are very wide and they are free of any means for zombies to reach down and grab at them (such as from bridges). Humans in turn depend on access to LOCs to evacuate from zones of zombie incursion and to ensure the delivery of goods necessary to survive during a zombie attack.

Operational COG #2: Potable Water sources (PWS)

Zombies do not drink water, but humans do. Humans typically cannot survive longer than 10 days without fresh water. Zombies will likely be drawn to water sources by the presence of human food sources that zombies prey on. Zombies can be expected to contaminate potable water sources with various contaminants during these attacks, further limiting the supply of available potable water for humans.

DECISIVE POINTS/CRITICAL CAPABILITIES (CCs)

The following Critical Capabilities (CC) are crucial enablers for the strategic and operational centers of gravity to function. As such, they are essential to the accomplishment of this plan's objectives.

CC #1—Medical Infrastructure:

Zombie interactions will create human casualties who will eventually become zombies depending upon the source of the zombieism. In cases where zombieism manifests slowly, injured humans will likely seek out medical care in hospitals and local clinics. These locations will ultimately become sources of zombieism in and of themselves as victims mutate. Not only will this render hospitals useless, it will likely cause irreparable casualties among medical professionals and members of the Chaplain Corps who will be necessary to combat zombie dominance. Further, zombies in hospitals will deny healthy humans access to medical equipment, medicines and blood/tissue/organ banks necessary for survival. An increase in the number of zombie casualties will have a direct impact on the number of personnel flooding LOCs to evade zombies. Further, damage to medical infrastructures will likely degrade the abilities of healthy human populations to purify potable water sources.

CC #2—Law Enforcement Infrastructure:

Zombie interactions will elicit call outs for law enforcement forces who will likely become casualties as a result of insufficient training/equipment for zombie threats. Law enforcement personnel will be essential to the maintenance of law, order, and security as humans evacuate from areas at risk of zombie invasion. Further law enforcement personnel will be essential to providing security for key resources (food and water distribution points, "safe" medical care facilities, transit choke points such as bridges and bus depots, and emergency evacuation sites). Humans facing zombies are likely to raid police stations, National Guard armories and other sporting goods stores in an attempt to arm themselves. A resultant breakdown in law and order will create conditions that will make it impossible to keep lines of communication operable or to mount an effective, unified action to counter zombie dominance.

CC #3—Power Distribution Infrastructure:

Power generation and transport infrastructures require significant maintenance and supervision performed by humans in order to remain within normal operating parameters. If humans responsible for these activities cannot perform them, then these infrastructures will begin to malfunction and their resulting failures will have a cascading effect that will quickly undermine law and order and the delivery of basic services that healthy human populations rely on. It is possible that the noises, lights or thermal emissions generated by these facilities will attract zombies and subsequently place human personnel working inside at considerable risk. If possible, remote-controlled robots should be utilized to operate and repair these infrastructure elements in lieu of humans. Further, damage to power infrastructures will likely degrade the abilities of healthy human populations to maintain potable water sources or operate LOCs effectively.

DECISIVE POINTS/CRITICAL REQUIREMENTS (CR)

The following Critical Requirements (CR) are essential conditions, resources, and means for the critical capabilities in this plan to be fully operational.

CR #1—Effective Emergency Triage/Quarantine Procedures:

Promptly identifying humans contaminated by a source of zombieism and subsequently isolating them from the healthy population will be essential factors with regard to keeping hospitals and medical infrastructures in operation. Casualties contaminated by zombie sources must not be allowed to interact with healthy humans. Affected humans must be quarantined and subsequently eradicated. Failure to establish these conditions will undermine all CCs listed in this plan.

CR #2—Local/Tribal/State/Federal Emergency Management Integration:

Effective communications between local, tribal, state and federal law enforcement (LEL) and emergency management (EM) agencies will be essential to a concerted effort to secure healthy human populations and the resources they depend on from zombie domination. As stated in the 9/11 Commission Report, LE and EM entities at all levels require interoperable communications equipment, HAZMAT decontamination equipment, comparable training standards and coordination procedures. Gaps and Seams between these entities will create conditions that will undermine all the CCs in this plan.

CR #3—Effective Infrastructure Security:

If energy, water, or sewage/sanitation infrastructures are compromised by zombies, conditions will be created that could undermine law and order and induce systematic failures in medical and water distribution capabilities. Further, in the case of sewage and sanitation infrastructures, if zombies compromise these capabilities, conditions will exist that will facilitate the spread of disease and pathogen-harboring parasites. In addition, compromise to these capabilities will jeopardize food and water sources for healthy humans and other wildlife and fauna that could prove key to survival. If compromised, the capabilities in this CR could undermine all the CCs in this plan.

CR #4—Safe food, water, and fuel distribution network:

Ultimately, healthy human populations and the forces protecting them will require the means to acquire, purify, and distribute foodstuffs, water and fuels for heat and machine operations. Failure to maintain security supporting the distribution networks and nodes for food, water and fuel will compromise the longevity of healthy humans; decrease the amount of time that humans can remain sheltered in place or barricaded from zombie threats and could cause competition for resources that will undermine law and order. If compromised, the capabilities in this CR could undermine all the CCs in this plan.

CR #5—Effective Threat Surveillance and Warning Program:

Government agencies at all levels must possess an effective means to communicate information about zombie outbreaks, potential zombie contamination vectors, and the safety/security of critical support infrastructures and LOCs within their areas of operations. Absent an effective surveillance program, zombie forces could mass before an effective response could be mounted by healthy humans to counter zombie dominance. Failure to institute an effective surveillance and warning program as outlined in this CR could undermine all the CCs in this plan.

FRIENDLY ELEMENTS

Federal Departments and Agencies

US Department of State (DoS). The Secretary of State (primarily through USAID/OFDA) is responsible for coordinating international preparation and response to include persuading other nations to join our efforts to contain or slow the spread of a zombie phenomenon, limiting the adverse impacts on trade and commerce, and coordinating efforts to assist other nations impacted by zombie phenomena. DoS is also responsible for interaction with all American citizens overseas.

US Department of Defense

a. **The Office of the Secretary of Defense (OSD).** OSD is the principal staff element of the Secretary of Defense in the exercise of policy development, planning, resource management, and program evaluation responsibilities.

b. **The Under Secretary of Defense for Personnel and Readiness (USD P&R).** USD P&R leads Force Management Policy, Reserve Affairs, Health Affairs, Readiness, and Program Integration.Force Management Policy assesses and manages the force and Health Affairs is responsible for sustaining the health of the service members and their families. Reserve Affairs is responsible for preparing reserve forces and Readiness is responsible for overall force readiness. Program Integration is responsible for integrating crosscutting functions across P&R.

c. **The Assistant Secretary of Defense for Health Affairs (ASD(HA)).** ASD (HA) serves as the principal medical advisor to the SecDef, providing policy and guidance for health services supporting service members during military operations. ASD (HA) establishes FHP guidelines and prioritizes distribution of vaccines and anti-viral medications by the Services in cooperation with the GCCs. ASD (HA) also develops policy for health civil-military operations, health stability operations, humanitarian assistance and disaster relief, and military health support to the interagency and NGOs. DoD components will ensure operational considerations are integrated with the FHP implementation measures directed in this CONPLAN. As a direct reporting unit to ASD (HA), the Armed Forces Health Surveillance Center (AFHSC) serves as the DoD center for comprehensive health surveillance information to include analysis, interpretation, and dissemination of information regarding the health of the US military and military-associated populations.

d. **The Assistant Secretary of Defense for Homeland Defense and Americas' Security Affairs (ASD (HD&ASA)).** The ASD (HD&A-SA) is designated by zombie phenomena effort, and provides policy oversight for civil support missions.

e. The Assistant Secretary of Defense for Public Affairs (ASD (PA)). The ASD (PA) is the principal advisor to SecDef for public affairs and the DoD focal point for zombie phenomena media queries.

f. The Office of the Chairman of the Joint Chiefs of Staff (OCJCS). The CJCS is the principal military advisor to the President and SecDef, and communicates SecDef guidance to the Combatant Commanders, Services, and DoD Agencies.

Other Supporting DoD Agencies

Defense Commissary Agency (DeCA). DeCA will support installation-level preparedness and zombie phenomena contingency response planning.

Defense Contract Management Agency (DCMA). DCMA deploys contingency contract administration services (CCAS) to the Area of Operations (AO) to administer civil augmentation programs (e.g., Army Logistics Civil Augmentation Program (LOGCAP) and the Air Forces Civil Augmentation Program (AFCAP)) external support contracts and weapons system support contracts with place of performance in theater when authority is delegated by the appropriate service contracting agency.

Defense Information Systems Agency (IDSA). DISA will ensure commands, services, and agencies receive timely and effective command, control, communications, computers, and intelligence (C4I) and other support.

Defense Intelligence Agency (DIA) National Center for Medical Intelligence (NCMI). NCMI will provide intelligence warning of diseases with epidemic or pandemic potential and provide intelligence assessments of the implications, outlook, and opportunities associated with the spread of a potentially epidemic or pandemic disease, to include zombie phenomena. NCMI will also provide intelligence warning and finished all-source medical intelligence analysis regarding foreign emerging/re-emerging infectious diseases (to include zombie phenomena) of operational significance to the Combatant Commanders, the DoD, and the US government as a whole. NCMI will provide information regarding foreign medical capability to plan for, report, identify, and respond to zombie phenomena threats.

Defense Logistics Agency (DLA). DLA coordinates with GCCs and Service components for medical, antiviral, PPE, subsistence, clothing, individual equipment, petroleum, construction materials, personal demand items, medical materials and repair parts support. DLA provides integrated material management and supply support for all DLA-managed material. DLA also provides property and hazardous material (HAZMAT) disposal services.

Defense Threat Reduction Agency (DTRA). DTRA provides modeling, hazard prediction, technical subject matter expertise, and planning support upon request of the supported commander. DTRA leverages its Biological Threat Reduction Program to strengthen state capabilities for bio-surveillance, early detection, and rapid response to human, animal and plant diseases of operational significance. DTRA also has the capability to provide hazardous avoidance mapping and Consequence Management Advisory Team (CMAT) support.

National Geospatial-Intelligence Agency (NGA). NGA provides geospatial intelligence (GEOINT) to include imagery, imagery intelligence, and geospatial information and service products data and associated services in support of zombie phenomena contingency response operations for DoD, primary agencies, and coordinating agencies as directed. As appropriate, NGA provides GEOINT release and disclosure guidance to supporting organizations.

DECISIVE POINTS/CRITICAL VULNERABILITIES (CV)

The following Critical Vulnerabilities (CV) are aspects of the critical requirements in this plan which are deficient or vulnerable to direct or indirect attack that will create decisive or significant effects.

CV #1—Individual Healthy Humans (IHH):

The IHH is the singlemost important factor shared by all the COGs, CCs, and CVs in this plan. A zombie outbreak can affect thousands of IHHs in the span of minutes. Ironically, given the consideration that zombie outbreaks in human hosts cannot possibly last longer than 40 days (because human hosts require food and water to continue functioning) there may be times when IHHs will be forced to abandon other IHHs who are unable to evade sources of zombie contamination. Such situations could arise while IHHs are evacuating in the face of incoming zombie forces. IHHs must not be allowed to "go back for" family, friends, or other personnel who cannot get away from zombies quickly enough. All IHHs who fall behind must be left behind. Such decisions are abhorrent to normal IHHs and military and LE personnel protecting them must rigidly enforce such restraint. Healthy humans can wait out a zombie outbreak if they are prudent. Nothing can be done to cure a human if they become a zombie. Every human that becomes a zombie increases the enemy's numbers and decreases the chances that healthy humans will survive.

REMAINDER OF PLAN UNDER WORK.

Members of several agencies of the Intelligence Community commented on the draft CONPLAN 8888. Here are some of their most notable observations:

- While we're all focused on zombies, the vampires and werewolves are out there getting stronger. This will all end in tears.
- Fortunately, the werewolves and vampires are too busy fighting each other to pose a significant threat. If they were ever to put aside their differences, however...
- Better stock up on garlic and silver bullets, just in case
- If I see a line in the budget to fund SPARKLCOM, I'm giving up. Just a heads-up.
- Counter-Zombie Dominance Operations: my new favorite catch phrase.

- Yeah, everybody thinks it's a joke—until you hear a knock on your door and some little zombie wants to sell you brain cookies! I'd probably buy 'em only because getting a real kid to the door selling crap is so rare.
- It's real. You can get brains to eat. Well, in Japan, at Capcom's bar that's opening up in Shinjuku. You can get a Resident Evil food item that looks like brains, but is in fact brains-shaped cake with some strawberry syrup on it to look like a little blood.
- I spotted a mistake in the plan. The Shortfalls section mentions a shortage of materials to form barriers against zombies; many of these would be ineffective, or less effective, against zombie enemies. Examples:
    - Sandbags are often intended to protect against enemy gunfire, which zombies do not use anyway.
    - Much of barbed wire's effectiveness in preventing enemy movement results from pain, which zombies are immune to. Similarly, zombies will not be deterred from moving across areas protected by barbed wire; are unlikely to suffer significant injuries from barbed wire (even losing fingers on concertina wire would only somewhat reduce a zombie's combat capability, and blood loss is generally irrelevant to zombies); and will not slow down to rescue any casualties that might occur.
    - Anti-personnel mines will inflict casualties on a zombie horde, but that is not actually the main purpose of a minefield. The main purpose of a minefield is to discourage movement across them, and mines will be completely ineffective in this against zombie hordes. (Indeed, a minefield can fail against a human enemy with large numbers that is willing to accept casualties.)
    - A minefield may still be useful as warning of zombie approaches. If zombies are attracted to noise, a minefield

might be used to channel a horde's movement *towards* the mines, but there are cheaper ways to produce noises to channel the movement of hordes.

- Riot control chemicals are likely to be completely ineffective against zombies.
- Note that all of these materials might be needed for the secondary purpose of deterring attacks by human mobs or militias.
- Well, this is still a "live" document, pardon the pun, so maybe you could send them recommendations for revisions.

- "Mister President! We simply cannot afford a Zombie Weaponization Gap!"
- Vampires and werewolves are nice suggestions for the next time they do this.
- I hereby suggest another scenario: the threat is the Death Eaters, a fascist terrorist group with very small numbers and little chance of further recruitment, but possessing capabilities which are impossible for US armed forces to duplicate, not least being mind control abilities, magical concealment techniques, and uninterceptable transportation/communication abilities. Further, their intended goal is the enslavement or extermination of nearly the entire population of the British Isles, if not further. If unopposed, the Death Eaters are likely to inflict casualties on a greater scale than Hitler or Stalin.
- The US has the advantage of their unfamiliarity with modern technology, but this advantage is likely to dissipate over time. Their unfamiliarity is ideologically-based, not intrinsic to the group. Death Eaters are capable of learning and using Muggle tech; at least the bulk of, and likely the entirety of, US armed forces are simply genetically incapable of using magic.

- Worse yet, the Death Eaters have already penetrated the UK government to an unknown extent (via the aforementioned mind control abilities). Muggle government is a low priority target for them for ideological reasons—but total control of the UK government is probably in their capabilities. Thus, the UK could not be considered reliable for support in operations on its own territory, and very well might be hostile. Even US forces currently located in the UK may be under their influence. Fortunately, it is fairly likely that the Death Eaters do not understand the full potential of the UK's weapons of mass destruction, and probably have not made them top priority for control as a more conventional foe would have. Also, the Death Eaters' numbers are so low (no more than a few hundred people), they are not believed to be operating outside the UK except maybe for one or two individual agents.
- For purposes of the plan, it can be assumed that Dumbledore's plan failed; or at best that the US is unaware of a magical faction opposing the Death Eaters.
- There. The students have to make a strategic plan for a poorly understood threat, with delicate political considerations in play. You might have to call them the Life Takers and their leader Baron Vandalor to avoid lawsuits, though.
- And oh yeah, NSA would be useful against the zombie hordes in *World War Z*. No comms equals no COMINT. No electronics equals no ELINT. We would still be needed to monitor other human governments, organized survivor/militia groups, and the like. For instance, in the actual *World War Z* book, Iran and Pakistan end up in a nuclear exchange after Iran tries to seal its border with Pakistan and border incidents escalate.
- Even orbital assets, however, should be able to detect and track the larger hordes. They would behave differently than a mob of refugee humans.

- For a while now, I've maintained that in the HP universe, there must be a contingent of American wizards in the IC; at the very last, someone has to edit out magical facilities from NTM imagery.
- Can we be certain that EMZ zombies will be more dangerous to atheists, or that the Chaplain Corps will have the best solutions to the EMZ problem? Various references do suggest the later (such as the British film *Plague of the Zombies*), but I don't know of much evidence of the former, although I have seen a film (*Dracula Has Risen from the Grave*) which suggests that vampires will be extra dangerous to atheists.
- A lot depends on how the EMZ are created. If they are made via Lovecrftian magic, involving horrible rugose entities or aelder epochs and non-Euclidean planes, the mathematicians and physicists employed by the US IC and allied ICs may be of more use: members of the British Rocket Group may be of especial use in this case.
- Personally I'm actually scared of Zombie Chickens.
- Plus I thought there was another form of Zombieism in nature. There's a wasp that's a parasite to another larger bug (I forgot which) and it eats part of the brain and it eventually takes control of the larger insect and directs its actions. I heard about it on RadioLab.
- Wasps are evil…

CLASSICAL JOKES

What does a spy do when he gets too cold? He goes undercover.

// 🌐 //

A guy driving in a rural area sees a sign that says "Talking Dog, $25." Intrigued, he drives up to the farmhouse and asks the farmer how he obtained the dog by his side. The farmer says, "I got it when I was with CIA. I was involved in all sorts of operations. I was in on the capture of Saddam Hussein. I was part of the operation that found bin Laden." The dog looks at the driver, and said, "He's lying. He never worked for the CIA."

// 🌐 //

FBI Guidance to Surveillants: You Know You've Been Burned When: . . The subject goes through a tollbooth, and when you arrive, the attendant says, "The driver ahead of you paid for you."

POLITICAL HUMOR FROM NORTH KOREA

Courtesy of Radio Free Asia

Ed's note: When I was interviewed on NPR while promoting the first volume of my spy humor series, I was stumped when Scott Simon asked, "Is there any North Korean humor?" Now, thanks to the crack research team of Radio Free Asia, I'm happy to report that there is.

Happy days

An Englishman, a Frenchman, and a North Korean are having a chat. The Englishman says: "I feel happiest when I'm at home, my wool pants on, sitting in front of the fireplace."

The Frenchman, a ladies' man, says: "You English people are so conventional. I feel happiest when I go to a Mediterranean beach with a beautiful blond-haired woman, and we do what we've got to do on the way back."

The North Korean man says: "In the middle of the night, the secret police knock on the door, shouting: Kang Sung-Mee, you're under arrest! And I say, Kang Sung-Mee doesn't live here, but right next door! That's when we're happiest!"

// 🌐 //

Long Live Kim Jong-Il!

Chang Man Yong works on a collective farm in North Korea. He goes fishing, gets lucky, and brings a fish home. Happy about his catch, he tells his wife: "Look what I've got. Shall we eat fried fish today?"

The wife says: "We've got no cooking oil!"

"Shall we stew it, then?"

"We've got no pot!"

"Shall we grill it?"

"We've got no firewood!"

Chang Man Yong gets angry, goes back to the river, and throws the fish back into the water. The fish, happy to have had such a narrow escape, sticks its head out of the water and cheerfully yells: "Long live General Kim Jong- Il!"

// 🌐 //

Move over, comrade!

(Ed's note: This is a variation on a Soviet-era joke.)

Two men are talking on a Pyongyang subway train:

How are you, comrade?"

"Fine, how are you doing?"

"Comrade, by any chance, do you work for the Central Committee of the Workers' Party?"

"No, I don't."

"Have you worked for the Central Committee before?"

"No, I haven't."

"Then, are any of your family members working for the Central Committee?"

"Nope."

"Then, get away from me! You're standing on my foot!"

// 🌐 //

Bear hug

Kim Jong-Il and Vladimir Putin are having a summit meeting in Moscow. During a break, they're bored, and they decide to bet to see whose bodyguards are more loyal.

Putin is on the 20th floor and calls on his bodyguard Ivan, opens the window, and says: "Ivan, jump!"

Sobbing, Ivan says: "Mr. President, how can you ask me to do that? I have a wife and child waiting for me at home."

Putin sheds a tear himself, apologizes to Ivan, and sends him away.

Next, it's Kim Jong-Il's turn. He calls his bodyguard Lee Myung-Man and yells: "Lee Myung-Man, jump!" Not hesitating for a split second, Lee Myung-Man is just about to jump out the window. Putin hugs Lee Myung-Man to prevent him from jumping and says: "Are you out of your mind? If you jump out this window, you'll die! This is the 20th floor!" Nevertheless, Lee Myung-Man is still struggling, trying to escape Putin's embrace and jump out the window: "President Putin, please let me go! I have a wife and child at home!"

// 🌐 //

Out of the mouths...

At High School No. 1 in Pyongyang, a girl brags to her teacher about the cat she's got at home: "Our cat has just given birth to seven kittens. All of them just stick close to their mother, they feel really comfortable, and sleep all the time. They're all true communists."

A few days later, the teacher asks the girl: "Are the communist kittens at home growing up nicely?"

The girl says: "Comrade teacher, big trouble! They've all opened their eyes, and they've all renounced communism!"

// 🌐 //

Looking at the sun and saying it is the moon

Child: "Mom, I'm hungry. I want rice."

Mother: "I'm sorry, child. There's no rice left."

Child: "No rice! Why is there no rice? Our kindergarten teacher told us that if General Kim Jong-Il points his finger to sand, it turns into rice. So, why is there no rice in our house?"

Mother: "Well, that's a lie. No, what I actually meant to say was that's a matter of deeply-rooted belief."

Child: "Mom, what's deeply-rooted belief?"

Mother: "Well, it's a lie you're supposed to believe."

// 🌐 //

Another country

A woman living in North Hamgyong province returns home after a hard day at the open market. While she was working hard, the husband spent the whole day at home, daydreaming. As soon as she returns home, they start talking, and the husband says: "Sweetheart, I'd love to go to some place I've never seen before, and do something I've never done before…"

The wife retorts: "That's a great idea. Go to the kitchen and wash the dishes!"

Black cats, white cats, large mice

Chinese, Russian, Japanese, American, and North Korean police officers gather and decide to assess their investigative capacity. Under the watchful eye of their supervisors, each team gets a mouse, then lets it loose, and the mouse runs up a big mountain. The winning team is the one that manages to catch and bring back the mouse in the shortest time.

The Chinese police employ human wave tactics, combing every square inch on the mountain in their thousands.

They capture and return the mouse after only one day's search.

The Japanese policemen use a smell detector, and after only half a day, they detect the mouse hole, search it, catch the mouse and bring it back.

The Russian cops send a robot equipped with a heat-seeking device up the mountain. The robot locates all the mammals on the mountain and after only three hours the Russians capture and bring back the mouse.

The only ones left now are the American and North Korean police officers. The Americans use a satellite signal device to locate the mouse, and then send in a mechanical gadget that looks like a snake gliding up the mountain.

The gadget gets into the mouse hole, catches the mouse and brings it back after only one hour.

The North Koreans are last. Although the supervisors are watching, none of them makes a move, there is no brainstorming, and no one comes up with a plan of action, nothing at all. After only about 10 minutes, a few

North Korean police officers show up dragging a dog before the supervisors, saying they've found the mouse.

All the supervisors are puzzled: "What are you doing? It is not a dog you were supposed to catch! Weren't you supposed to catch a mouse?" Instead of answering, the North Korean cops drag the dog through the dirt and repeatedly kick it in the ribs. The sobbing dog suddenly starts to talk: "Stop, stop, please stop! Yes, I confess, I'm a mouse! I'm a mouse, please concede that I'm a mouse, or else they're going to kill me!"

// 🌐 //

Food for thought

Professor: "Comrade students, how many economic-political systems are there in the world?"

Student: "There are three such systems: The capitalist economic-political system, the North Korean socialist economic system, and the Chinese eclectic system."

Professor: "Then, among these three systems, which one is the greatest?"

Student: "Well, it might be rather difficult to answer that question."

Professor: "What kind of an answer is that? There is only one clear answer! Our style of socialist economic-political system is the greatest, as this is the system that's destined to conquer the entire world and spur eternal economic development!"

Student: "Professor, that is great, indeed… But if our system takes over the world and all of the other countries and economic-political systems, then whom are we going to ask for food aid?"

// 🌐 //

Black and white

A member of the Chinese Communist Party goes to study in North Korea, where he gets to learn about juche, the official state ideology of North Korea and the political system based on it.

The Chinese Communist Party member wishes to let his friends back home know what life in North Korea is like.

However, he knows for sure that all the letters he sends are opened by the North Korean authorities, so he thinks of a way to bypass censorship.

The Chinese decides to write words meaning precisely what they say in blue ink, words conveying neutral meaning in black ink, and words intended to convey the very opposite meaning in green ink.

After a while, his friends back home in China receive a letter from North Korea. The letter was written entirely in black ink, meant for words carrying neutral meaning.

The conclusion they draw is that North Korea is not as good as the North Korean authorities' propaganda says it is, and it is not as bad as the critics of the North Korean regime say it is. However, at the bottom of the letter, they come across a note from their friend: "My friends, I apologize. Green ink is unavailable here."

//🌐//

The Workers' Paradise

At an art museum in Europe, an Englishman, a Frenchman, and a North Korean stand before a painting of Adam and Eve holding an apple in the Garden of Eden.

The Englishman says: "The man has something tasty to eat and is eager to share it with the woman. Based on that, I would conclude that they're rather obviously English."

The Frenchman says: "I disagree. They're walking around entirely naked, so they must be French."

The North Korean says: "There is no doubt in my mind that they're North Korean. They have no clothes to wear, barely anything to eat, and they still think they're in heaven!"

Original reporting in Korean by Jinseo Lee. RFA Korean service director: Kwang-Chool Lee. Translated by Grigore Scarlatoiu. Edited by Luisetta Mudie and Sarah Jackson-Han.

THE TERRORISM REVUE

Ed's Note: Various Intelligence Agency organizations provide periodic updates on terrorist groups, attacks, and countermeasures. One of the earliest was the *Terrorism Review*, here parodied. This version was stamped Directorate of Ignorance, Sacred Noforn Nocontent, Arcane, April 1, 1985, GITR 85-007. It came replete with a Table of Contents and a note from the publisher: "The Terrorism Revue of 1 April is published annually on 1 April. Copies may be obtained gratis from any branch of Rote Hilfe. If you do not know what Rote Hilfe is, much less where to find one of its branches, it means the system is working." (Rote Hilfe was a left-wing German prisoner support group affiliated with the International Red Aid and the Communist Party of Germany.) I've corrected a few unintentional typos, but left intact the intentional ones.

Focus: New Wrinkles in Terrorism

<u>Dirtballs out</u>: The latest word in terrorism? Guerrilla fashions. Gone are the days of dowdy, Castroite fatigues. Dirtball appearances have become outre. Unkempt, filthy, disheveled activists are now considered gauche in prominent terrorist circles. As terrorists seek new supporters among the former radicals of the 1960s who have become today's yuppies and preppies, a new trend in terrorist tactics has emerged—trendy gaudery.

Socks off: Terrorists are wowing the public with a new image and absolutely knocking the socks off the tellers in the banks they rob. Guerrilla leaders recently spotted in Georgetown were sporting hand-painted tee-shirts with catchy Marxist or Maoist slogans, brightly-colored bandanas, and the latest denims from Bill Blast. Italian terrorists interviewed in Milan last week claimed credit for the swift upsurge in the hot, radical clothing. "Business is just bombing," one remarked. Middle Eastern radicals, not to be outdone, have shed their raghead image for an updated version of the classic Lebanese tunic matched with mukluks imported from Greenland.

Uzis kicky: Word has it, nevertheless, that the basic "little black hood" will always be in good taste, especially when matched with a silvertone tie and a kicky Uzi or Kalashnikov.

HIGHLIGHTS

Alert Items

The Free World: Terrorist Merger Overwhelms Western Alphabet

On 1 April, according to a source of undetermined reliability quoting a subsource of questionable access, the innocuously named Armenian Boys Choir (ABC), a terrorist splinter of the reactionary Dashnak Extremist Fighters for God, Homeland, Independence, and Justice (DEFGHIJ), has merged with the Kurdish Liberation Movement of November One (KLMNO) and the Pro-Qadhafi Revolutionary Secessionists of Turkey (PQRST) to form the Union of Violent Warriors (UVW). An earlier report from an obviously demented Middle Eastern liaison contact that the Xenophobic Youth of Zimbabwe (XYZ) had also joined the new alliance has proved to be hogwash. Nevertheless, the merger threatens terrorist analysts in all Western countries because it has used up almost all the letters of the alphabet. As usual, there is absolutely no evidence that the Soviet Union instigated this development. On the other hand, surely it is no coincidence that the Cyrillic alphabet was untouched.

United Kingdom: ARM Opuns Terrier Campaign to Hamstering Animal Abusers

On 1 April at a press conference in Bathwater, the Animal Rights Militia (ARM) announced it is dogtired of pussyfooting around and will kill humans who abuse animals. The fetching ARM spokeswoman, an otter ARM terrorist standing rat at her side, said, "Hare this warning: we ant kidding; anyone who frogets or gerbils my message is an ass." "I smell something fishy," mused one reported; "This monkey business bears more study. Tell us what your real porpoise is," he shouted, horsely. The newshound beside him retorted, "Ewe bee krait! Swan thing to be skeptical, but moose you badger the gorilla my dreams? She's just promoting eagle opportunity for animals. Llama tell you heron now, it's a whale of a story."

United States: New Terror Threat to American Way

On 1 April, the previously un-heard of "Cabbage Patch Doll Liberation Front" (CPDLF) demanded improved accommodations and meals both in retail establishments and in homes, in addition to three weeks of annual leave and cost of living raises, or it would begin trashing toy stores, beginning with the infamous "Toys R Us". It is believed that counterfeit dolls smuggled in from Iran and North Korea aboard Libyan ships with Cuban and Nicaraguan crews at Soviet behest are behind this subversive thrust at the holy Christmas shopping season.

International: PLO To Resume Terrorism

In the wake of Jordanian King Hussein's decision, announced 1 April, to travel to Jerusalem next week to sign a peace treaty with Israel, and Israel's concomitant offer to establish and support an independent Palestinian state on the West Bank with Jerusalem as its capital, PLO leader Yasir Arafat has instructed the Fatah loyalists (all six who remain) to form a group to launch terrorist strikes against Western and moderate Arab countries. "This development threatens the entire basis of the Palestinian movement, not to mention my job," Arafat reported asserted. The new group will be known as "Black April".

KEY INDICATORS

United Nations: Plans to Get Tough With Terrorists

On 1 April, ending more than 20 years of spineless indecisiveness, the UN General Assembly voted overwhelmingly in favor of a Swedish resolution to form a multilateral armed force dedicated to executing preemptive and retaliatory strikes against terrorists. The force will be called the United Nations Counterterrorist Lethality Executor (UNCLE). China will provide five battalions of crack ground troops; the Soviet Union will supply aircraft (to be flown by Togolese pilots); Vietnam and Iraq will furnish poison gas. Poland's offer of 100 mounted cavalry officers was politely refused. The US offer of tactical nuclear weapons was taken under advisement.

The establishment of UNCLE met a mixed reception in the Real World:

Yasir Arafat declared, "The PLO applauds this effort to bring peace to the Middle East and other troubled areas of the world. Fatah declares its willingness to join forces to combat the extremists who shamelessly try to exploit minor cultural and religious differences for selfish personal or political gain."

The Ayatollah Khomeini responded, "In the name of Allah, the merciful, the compassionate. This plot of the imperialistic Zionistic cabal will not hinder the righteous cause of Islam, which will triumph over the puny, morally decadent lickspittles of the Great Satan. In other words, stick it in your hairy ear."

The Vatican: Counterterrorist Strike Force Organized

The growing support for liberation theology in Latin America and Western Europe has forced the Vatican to rethink its original, pre-Council of Trent, counterterrorist strategy. According to a faithful source, officers within the inner recesses of the Vatican's notorious Propaganda Fide (Defense Of The Faith, or DOTF), have agreed to form a new counterterrorist strike unit to be called the Defenders of the One True Church (DOTC). The elite, paramilitary fighting force will be composed entirely of battle-hardened ex-fifth-grade nuns, trained and led by Jesuit paramilitary officers. DOTC will be used to combat "subversive and heretical tendencies—that is, terrorism—within the Church."

The hooded, black-robed leader of the group, identified only as the Right Reverend Field-Marshall, asserted at a press conference in Rome that henceforth all heretics—in other words, terrorists—will either be shot or excommunicated, adding that in his opinion the former was preferable, since "Anathema, extra ecclesiam, nula sanctam". ("Outside the Church, there is no salvation.") Upon hearing these words, one reporter present at the press conference was moved to exclaim, "Fidem Scit!" ("He knows his faith.") whereupon he was ejected by a Swiss Guard who did not understand Latin.

The Vatican: Carlos To Take the Cloth?

On 1 April, according to unimpeachable Vatican sources, the infamous international terrorist Carlos, who has for years headed a small band of intrepid leftwing dirtbags, was granted an audience with Pope John Paul II, during which he confessed his sins, received absolution from the Pontiff, and decided to take Holy Orders. After cleaning up some unfinished personal business in Damascus, the Vatican sources added, Carlos will travel to a Carmelite monastery in Israel to begin his religious studies. The audience with the Pope was three times the normal length, the source said, because it took Carlos so long to list his sins. "But he felt much better afterward."

Cuba: Radical Entente Members Confer

On 1 April in Havana, according to bearded sources, Cuban leader Fidel Castro hosted a gathering of senior military and intelligence officials from Iran, Syria, North Korea, Bulgaria, Libya, and Nicaragua. They participated in an intensive round of discussions, special forces demonstrations, and inspection of recent developments in small surface-to-air missiles. A Soviet major general from the KGB's 8th Department reportedly attended as an observer. In the absence of additional data, we tend to discount rumors that joint terrorist operations may have been discussed. Economic cooperation, cultural exchanges, and discussion of strategies to promote peaceful disarmament probably occupied center stage.

Syria: Carlos To Turn Capitalist?

On 1 April, infamous international terrorist Ilich Ramirez Sanchez, better known as Carlos, who has for years headed a small band of intrepid leftwing terrorist scuzzballs, announced at a press conference in Damascus that he had decided to form a company to market Cabbage Patch dolls worldwide. Syrian President Assad will resign his office to accept a position as Chief Executive Officer of the company. Libyan leader Muammar Qadhafi will also resign his office to become Director Sales Promotion of the new company. Carlos indicated Qadhafi plans to implement an imaginative new scheme he has dubbed "coercive marketing", drawing upon his long years of experience in international public relations.

Asked by reporters whether there was any truth to previous stories that, after a meeting with Pope John Paul II, he was renouncing terrorism and would join the priesthood, Carlos replied, "Are you gringos out of your gourds?"

SIGNIFICANT DEVELOPMENTS

France: Corsica Vaporized in Apparent FNLC Mishap

On 1 April, the entire island of Corsica suddenly disappeared in a thunderous explosion heard as far away as Butte, Montana. The ensuing tsunami tossed an estimated 350,000 tons of confused fish as far as 15 kilometers inland from Mediterranean beaches. The pall of dust caused by the explosion has permeated the stratosphere, which explains why it is so dark and cold now. According to Carl Sagan, in fact, we are all going to die in the coming "Corsican Winter". The cause of the explosion has not been established, but a French police official theorized that someone in the central bomb-making laboratory of the separatist National Front for the Liberation of Corsica (FNLC) probably dropped something he shouldn't have. "C'est la vie," he sighed, sipping his Pernod pensively.

France: Action Directe Soon To Be Eating Better

On 1 April, Jean Marc Rouillan and several other male members of the leftwing terrorist group Action Directe kidnapped Pierre Francois, head of the world-famous Cordon-Bleu cooking school. In a subsequent communique claiming responsibility for the act, Action Directe emphasized that no harm would come to Francois as long as he provided the group with fluffy souffles, flaky croissants, and savory sauces while he taught Nathalie Menigon, leader of the Action Directe Ladies Auxiliary, how to improve her atrocious cooking.

Italy: Agca Exonerates Bulgaria, Implicates Denmark

On 1 April, would-be assassin of Pope John Paul II Mehmet Ali Agca changed his story for the 341st time, announcing that everywhere he had previously said "Bulgaria" he had really meant "Denmark". Asked how he had come to make such a mistake, Agca said it had just been a slip of the tongue. "I was under a lot of pressure," he said, defensively. Asked why his latest testimony should now be believed, he replied, "You'll just have to trust me."

Spain: National Outcry Forces Police to Release Arrested Terrorists

On 1 April, Spanish authorities captured three of the most wanted members of the Military wing of the Spanish Basque terrorist group Basque Fatherland and Liberty (ETA/M). The three were surrounded by police and arrested without a struggle after they had interrupted their escape from the scene of a kidnaping in order to take their usual daily siesta at a highway rest stop. At the same time, police rescued the kidnap victim, a wealthy counterfeiter of Levis Action Slacks.

This noteworthy achievement went for naught, however, as soon as it became known that the police had conducted the operation during the sacred siesta period. The resultant outcry and public condemnation extended to the highest levels of the Spanish Government, forcing the police not only to release the three terrorists immediately, but also to compensate them with a free one-week vacation in Mallorca.

United Kingdom: Another al-Zoomphical Operation Foiled

On 1 April in London, nine members of the Pakistani terrorist group al-Zoomphical were arrested as they prepared to kidnap participants at a Rastafarian religious ceremony in Hyde Park. The head of the group, a swarthy, bearded, turbaned individual carrying a forged British passport in the name of Chauncey Edgar Honeycutt, confessed its goal had been to obtain hostages to trade for al-Zoomphical leader Slant Doornail Singh Bendawhale, who is languishing in a Karachi prison. "Honeycutt" admitted that the group, composed largely of illiterate Islamabad carwash employees, had mistaken the ceremony for an open-air reception of the US Embassy and had been hoping to seize some American diplomats. "We plan to keep doing this until we get it right," he asserted. Al-Zoomphical wages worldwide combat against what it terms the "Global Izodist Conspiracy", which it alleges is headed by Prince Charles, Lyndon Larouche, Cheryl Tiegs, and (of course) Abu Nidal.

Lebanon: Islamic Jihad Unmasked

On 1 April, a terrified customer of Honest Abdul's Auto Emporium in West Beirut sought sanctuary at the residence of the US Ambassador to Lebanon, current site of the US Embassy. He implored the US Government to protect him from the West Beirut Used Car Dealer's Association (UCDA), which had offered him the awful choice between driving a car bomb into a designated target building and accepting an American used car, with its inevitably crushing maintenance problems.

The fugitive revealed that the UCDA has been the guiding force behind the recent rash of car bombings in Beirut and other parts of Lebanon, the motive being to create a scarcity of used cars and thereby drive up the prices. "Shee-it, they ain't no Shi'ites," he said, explaining that the name Islamic Jihad was just a cover for the UCDA. As for the kidnap victims, he added, they were all people who had fallen behind on their car payments. The US Embassy rejected his request for asylum on the grounds that, by his own testimony, he was not a political refugee. As he departed, he vowed to die rather than accept an American used car. "And when I go," he added, "I'm going to take a bunch of you bastards with me."

Lebanon: Mercedes Winning Car Bomb War

According to the popular Lebanese magazine Car Bomb and Driver, Mercedes Benz sedans were involved in 54 percent of all terrorist incidents. The Mercedes 300SE and 280 Turbodiesel sedans, both of which can accommodate nearly 500 kilograms of explosives, were the most popular models, with the sporty 450SEL used only infrequently, probably owing to its limited cargo capacity. The most popular colors were lemon fester, sea phlegm, aqua-mucus, and emerald smear royale.

Volvos and Hondas were the closest competitors to the Mercedes, followed by another top-of-the-line West German car, the BMW, which is growing in popularity owing to its unexcelled ability to maneuver around obstacles. Toyotas, Nissans, and other Japanese cars also made a respectable showing, according to the magazine. Renaults, Fiats, Czech-made Skodas, and Soviet-made Ladas had their supporters as well. American cars, as usual, brought up the rear. Prospective suicide drivers reportedly have balked consistently at ending their lives in anything made in Detroit.

Libya: Qadhafi To Step Down

On 1 April, in an interview with a female Italian journalist noted for her big mouth and chest, Libyan leader Muammar Qadhafi revealed he has decided to resign his government position to pursue an unspecified business opportunity. Speaking from his tent in the desert outside Sirte, Qadhafi expressed an intention to improve his quality of life. "You think I am fool? Why you think I make treaties with Malta and Morocco? You see palm trees with well-developed beaches and females on them here? I am sick of trying to live up to reputation the Americans saddle me with. I am tired of same old camel race. I build villa and private airport in Malta and Marrakesh. Piss on the pipples. Piss on the Revolutionary Committees. Let them read Green Book, I'm going to read Hustler."

Jamaica: Soviets Ejected from SST Conference

On 1 April, the first annual Conference of State Supporters of Terrorism (SST) convened at a ganja plantation outside Kingston. Such mainstream SST superstars as Iran, Syria, and Libya were represented by strong delegations, but the Ayatollah Khomeini, expected to give the keynote address, begged off, electing instead to compete in the inaugural Qum Muslim Marathon.

The US delegation, composed of officials of the State Department Office for the Coordination of Terrorism Policy (M/CTP) expressed gratification for the international recognition accorded the "relatively modest contributions" of the United States in the SST field.

The US delegation also led a successful challenge in the SST Credentials Committee against the seating of the Soviet delegation. According to a senior official who sat next to the head of the US delegation even when he went to the bathroom but who may not be further identified, "The intelligence people have persuaded me that the Soviets have nothing to do with terrorism, and in my opinion this is just another example of them sticking their noses in where they're not wanted."

Peru: Pro-smoking Terrorist Groups Unite

The ruthless pro-smoking terrorist group Sendero Fuminoso (Smoking Path) and the urban-based Tupaca Marlboro group have joined forces in a collaborative effort to eliminate anti-smoking government forces throughout the three Emergency No-Smoking Zones recently established by the Peruvian President under the influence of Commie Pinko Yuppie liberal bed-wetting quiche-eating white-wine-sucking cabinet advisors. It remains to be seen if the unified front really does result, in the words of one local authority Chief Corruption Minister Ramon Allones Garcia y Vega y El Producto (popularly known as El Rum Soaked Crook), "the largest, single, pro-smoking, anti-clean-air, terrorist network in all of northeastern South America (hic)".

Japan: New Truck-Mounted Flamethrower Strikes Unexpected Target

On 1 April, when the extreme leftwing terrorist group Choo-choo-ha-ha (Inside Central Middle Core Nuclear Faction), unveiled its newest truck-mounted improvised flame projection device, a modified Saturn-5 booster rocket, flames from the rocket motors ignited fires that, as planned, destroyed the entire city of Tokyo. Unexpectedly, however, the flames spread to the set of the new motion picture being filmed outside the city: "Godzilla Meets the Abu Nidal Group". Godzilla was reportedly very annoyed, and Abu Nidal wasn't too pleased, either. Choo-choo-ha-ha has nervously offered profuse apologies.

Philippines: Moro Terrorists Commit Mass Suicide

On 1 April in Solo, more than 200 members of the Moro National Liberation Front (MNLF) committed suicide rather than spend another day with the foreign captive, a CIA terrorism analyst with a maddening propensity to commit puns. Over the five-month period the group had held the analyst hostage, it had gradually reduced its ransom demands, only to be told in the end, "Frankly, we wouldn't take him back if you paid us." The last words on a tape recording of the final grisly minutes of the group were uttered by guerrilla leader Taco Burpee Muhammad, who said, "We can't take any more of those Sikh jokes," just before delivering a Jonestown-style coup-de-grace to his equally exasperated followers. The CIA analyst was the only person left alive; unfortunately, he was shot to death by Philippine troops when they stormed the camp later the same day in an effort to rescue him.

Euroterrorist Alliance Disintegrates

On 1 April, the French leftwing terrorist group Action Directe and the Belgian group Communist Combatant Cells (CCC) announced in communiques found simultaneously in fortune cookies served in Chinese restaurants in Paris and Brussels that they had decided to dissolve their alliance with West Germany's Red Army Faction (RAF). The reason given was the RAF's "incredible operational failure rate," a fact the other two groups admitted they had not realized when they agreed to combine forces with the debonair, smooth-talking Germans. Specifically cited were the following:

- In 1976, the RAF operation to destroy the Office of the Attorney General in Karlsruhe using an improvised rocket launcher failed when a short circuit prevented any of the rockets from firing.
- In 1976, the RAF terrorists who occupied the West German Embassy in Stockholm emplaced explosives in preparation for blowing up the chancery if it was stormed, then set them off by accident so that they were forced to flee into the arms of the authorities.

- In 1977, the RAF operation to abduct financier Juergen Ponto to serve as a high-level hostage to swap for RAF prisoners failed when the would-be kidnapers neglected to consider he might be armed, and they ended up murdering him instead.
- In 1977, the PFLP-SOG hijacking of a Lufthansa airliner in sympathy with the RAF ended abruptly when the fledgling West German counterterrorist squad GSG-9 successfully stormed the plane, showing that RAF ineptitude is catching. "Es hat meinen Tag gemacht," remarked GSG-9 commander Uwe Wegener.
- In 1980, the RAF operation to kill NATO Commanding General Haig by blowing up a mine as his car travelled over it failed when the person responsible for detonating the mine neglected to consider the speed Haig's car was travelling and missed it by 12 feet.
- In 1981, the RAF operation to kill USARUER Commanding General Kroesen failed when the person firing the anti-tank rocket neglected to realize Kroesen's driver would stop when the traffic light turned red.
- By 1982, the RAF had set up a complicated system of caches of its operational material. It then left a map in one cache showing the locations of all the other caches; the map was in code, but some words had carelessly been written in the clear. After a mushroom picker accidentally discovered the main cache, a local policeman deciphered the map code after only a couple of days of work, leading to the discovery of all but one of the other caches.
- In 1982, despite the publicity surrounding the capture of Brigitte Mohnhaupt and Adelheid Schultz when they tried to visit the staked-out main cache, a week later Christian Klar was captured while trying to visit another staked-out cache.
- In 1984, six RAF terrorists planning a new operational campaign in a safe apartment were captured after one of them

accidentally fired a pistol shot through the floor into the apartment below, causing the resident of the lower apartment to complain to police.

- In 1984, the RAF operation to bomb the NATO officers training school in Oberammergau failed when the improvised explosive device suffered a timer malfunction. The terrorist who planted the bomb aroused suspicion by driving onto the base but running away from it while dressed in an incorrect US Marine Corps uniform.
- In 1985, conversely, an RAF operation to destroy a major computer center failed when the bomb, being delivered in a perambulator, detonated prematurely, killing the male terrorist and injuring his female companion. Reportedly, the perambulator was also somewhat the worse for wear.

According to the joint statement of Action Directe and the CCC, more such instances could be cited except for limitations in the dissemination media (no more room inside the fortune cookies). The statement concluded with an observation attributed to Action Directe leader Jean Marc Rouillan, that "Those Germans are interesting to talk to and they mean well, but we just can't afford to be involved with people who have been so consistently inept for such a long period of time." No RAF spokesman could be reached for comment.

Western counterterrorism analysts believe that on balance this is a positive development. Although it had been hoped that RAF ineptitude would infect the other, obviously more professional terrorist groups, it was always possible that the famous Gallic efficiency would reform the sloppy Germans, heightening the threat. This way the West community can be assured of continuing to deal with West German terrorists who will remain intimately acquainted with the manifestations of Murphy's Law for which they have so become justly renowned.

<u>Italy: Terrorist Groups Vie for Credit</u>

On 1 April, a swarthy, dark-haired male suspected of being a Mediterranean-type person stole a sheet of postage stamps from a Post Office

counter in broad daylight. Claiming credit for the daring act were the following Italian groups, some of which have been heard of:

- Red Brigades
- Red Brigades Veneto Column
- Red Brigades Bologna Pedestal
- Prima Linea
- Prima Vera
- Fettucini Alfredo
- Third Position
- Fourth Position
- Cramped Position
- Fetal Position
- Missionary Position
- New Order
- Black Order
- Black Border
- Proletarian International Revolutionaries
- International Revolutionary Proletarians
- Proletarian Revolutionary Internationalists
- Committee of Concerned Leftists
- Committee to Liberate Concerned Leftists
- Committee of Concerned Liberators
- Revolting Leftwing Battalions
- Salvation Army
- Union of Progressive Calabrian Lefthanders
- Communists United Against Everything
- Autonomia
- Semiautonomia
- Ludwig

Italian authorities are taking all of these claims seriously. "You never know who will need stamps," a senior Carabinieri official was quoted as commenting. "Besides," he added, "Those people use so many names, how can we be expected to keep them all straight? Anyway, one name is as good as another. Aren't they all the same?"

The US Embassy speculated that Italian terrorist groups are having trouble obtaining credit. "Do you know how hard it is to open a simple charge account when you're under cover?" asked an attaché who did not wish to be identified, as he plucked a piece of lint from his immaculately creased gabardines while he and his interlocutor enjoyed an espresso at the Café de Paris, a short distance away from the imposing US Embassy chancery on the Via Veneto. "We in the Clandestine Service understand the problems of living in the shadows like these terrorists do."

The Socioeconomic Origins of Middle Eastern Terrorism

According to our records, over half of the major terrorist attacks abroad last year either occurred in the Middle East or were of Middle Eastern origin. Indeed, over the past 10 years, the share of Middle Eastern incidents has steadily grown. That region also lays claim consistently to the lion's share of high casualty terrorist atrocities occurring around the world. In addition, demographic studies show that six out of 10 indigenous Middle Eastern males now claim active membership in a group or organization espousing political violence as one of its tactics. (By comparison, precisely 17 sociopathic Marxist-Leninist anarchist millennialists accounted for 96 percent of all terrorism in Western Europe—the second most common venue for attacks.)

Terrorism: An Economic Response

Our analysis suggests that this trend toward bloodletting is not predominantly political or religious in origin. Instead, it represents a rational response on the part of native Middle Easterners to their region's climatic conditions combined with the unsurmountable economic competition posed by the Japanese, South Koreans, and Taiwanese. Put simply, most Middle Easterners would prefer to fight than work.

- Weather conditions in most Middle Eastern locales favor occupations requiring two hours or less of labor daily; otherwise, available water supplies are insufficient to replace lost precious bodily fluids. At the same time, inadequate precipitation precludes concentrated agriculture for export.

- Late developing economically, those Middle Eastern countries not able to support themselves through petroleum production have been consistently deterred from introducing heavy or medium manufacturing by the market power of the United States, West Germany, and, most recently and particularly, Japan and other oriental production powerhouses.
- In contrast, however, ample funding has been available from the Soviet Union and oil-rich Gulf states to support anti-Israeli violence. In turn, Western states like France and the United States have willingly funded efforts to thwart these purveyors of violence and to provide war relief. In consequence, per capita income in most of the Middle East—despite an unemployment rate exceeding 74 percent—is higher than that in all but a few of the most developed states of Europe and North America.

In response to these pressures, most males in those Middle Eastern states without major hydrocarbon resources have elected to pursue the traditional Bedouin model for the region. This, in our view, represents a rational economic choice. Studies confirm that a typical day in the life of a male Bedouin tribesman breaks down as follows: (Hours may not add up to 24 due to rounding error.)

10.0 hours	Sleeping; fornication (with wives).
7.1 hours	Lying beside tent in shade; cleaning rifle; prayer; fornication, (with nonwives, including females); playing Walkman
5.0 hours	Eating, chewing q'at, petting cat.
1.7 hours	Miscellaneous fighting; commission of atrocities; disciplining wives
0.2 hours	Personal hygiene, supervising wives in stable maintenance

In contrast, Bedouin females average six hours sleeping, 13 hours in household maintenance/child care, three hours mucking stables, and two hours fanning/dancing for husbands. Time spent fornicating is deemed insignificant. It is worth underscoring that less than two hours of a Bedouin's day is spent in any form of physical labor. Most Middle Easterners, indolent by nature and culturally familiar with the Bedouin model, have readily chosen to follow this path even today.

In consequence, most Middle Eastern states and their residents have also opted for terrorism. Those few that have eschewed this route—Saudi Arabia, Kuwait, Bahrain—have been able to exploit their oil wealth (of course, relying on European contractors to do the manual labor). But, as oil profits have diminished for states like Libya and Iran, these countries, too, have jumped on the terrorism gravy train. A variety of reliable sources report that the typical Lebanese Shi'ite or Palestinian fighter as well as the run of the mill Maronite Christian militiaman spends 1.7 hours daily engaging in firing his gun or bombing civilians, with the remaining time in sleep or leisure—just like his Bedouin models. In return, the modern terrorist is amply funded for his efforts—or, more aptly, his lack thereof—by various Western and East Bloc powers anxious to prevent each other from dominating the region's oil wealth. It is no accident that most anti-Arab terrorism originates with Sabras, those Israelis most culturally connected with the Bedouin tradition. Conversely, Arab and Islamic elements permanently resident outside the Middle East—in parts of Europe, Asia, and North America—have been far less susceptible to the urge to commit atrocities, and instead have focused their efforts on retail enterprises and food service.

<u>Prospects</u>

Frankly, we believe prospects for any diminution of Middle Eastern terrorism are increasingly bleak. Not only is the terrorist life style a direct response to the economic realities of the region but it is rewarding in other ways as well. Moreover, based on our customary unsupported conjecture, we seriously doubt that any solution to the Palestinian problem, nor even the elimination of the Khomeini regime, would provide more than a short-term palliative for the region's ills.

At best some combination of the following events might at least serve to moderate the problem:

- Detonation of numerous thermonuclear devices approximately over the land mass of the Western Soviet Union,

Bulgaria, and Greece so as to alter Middle Eastern weather patterns. This approach would have additional obvious benefits as well.

- Relocation of the state of Israel and major Christian and Judaic Holy Land sites to an analogous climatic region, namely western Texas. Terrorism would, of course, continue but would be offset by an increase in revenues from pilgrims and tourists and a decrease in boredom (the bane of western Texas).
- A major increase in fossil fuel consumption by developed nations so as to raise the profitability of minor oil and gas fields in marginal Middle Eastern producing states like Syria.

Some analysts have suggested that such a combination of eventualities might entail certain consequences conceivably prejudicial to long-term Western interests, and that in addition certain ethical considerations militate against their implementation. Pay no attention to these sniveling quiche-eating white-wine-sucking toe-clenching liberal comsymp environmentalist pussies.

Abu Nidal: How He Does It

In recent months, the US Intelligence Community has encountered some difficulty in sorting out conflicting reports concerning the status, whereabouts, and activities of the notorious Palestinian terrorist and gadfly Sabri Khalil al-Banna, better known as Abu Nidal. Following are some typical reports:

- On 6 March, a French journalist interviewed Abu Nidal in the Bekaa Valley of Lebanon, according to an article he subsequently published in the leftwing French magazine *Le Canard Roti*. This was the first sighting by a Western (therefore trustworthy) observer of Abu Nidal since he died of a heart attack in Baghdad last October.
- Also on 6 March, Abu Nidal held a press conference in Tripoli attended by 37 Western (therefore truthful and objective) newspaper reporters.

- On 12 March, French police officials discounted the French journalist's claim that he had interviewed Abu Nidal. They suggested he had been the victim of a hoax by the Abu Nidal Group. (Formerly known as the Black June Organization (BJO), Fatah—the Revolutionary Council (F-TRC), the Arab Revolutionary Brigades (ARB), and the Shadowy Lebanese Union of Revolutionary Palestinians (SLURP).)
- On 20 March, opinionated sources reported Abu Nidal was "definitely dead" and could not be reached for comment, much less be interviewed by a French journalist. Furthermore, the sources added, Abu Nidal had been dead for some time, a fact that should have been evident to any interviewer.
- On 26 March, Abu Nidal was spotted at a seedy motel outside Orlando, Florida, holding discussions with persons later identified as officials of Disney World.
- On 30 March, pursuant to a request from his widow, Abu Nidal's perfectly preserved body was exhumed from its crypt in a mausoleum outside Baghdad and shipped via Purolator Courier to Lexington, Kentucky, where it was to be readied for the first post-mortem heart transplant operation in this century. The presiding surgeon is reportedly named something like Dr. Flankenstone.
- On 1 April, Abu Nidal was reportedly singed in a fire while making a movie with Godzilla outside Tokyo.

The Explanation

According to a sensitive and emotional source, Abu Nidal is indeed dead. Before he died, however, scientists used hairs from his moustache and clippings from his fingernails to clone exact replicas. Leading the surgical team was the world-renowned plastic surgeon Dr. Josef Mengele. The operation reportedly took place in a US Army hospital in West Germany.

This would explain why Abu Nidal was able to give an interview from the Bekaa Valley to a French journalist at the same time he was appearing on Libyan television with Colonel Qadhafi in Tripoli. This would also explain why the descriptions of the terrorists responsible for the recent simultaneous attacks on Turkish airlines offices in Rome, Athens, and Nicosia were so remarkably similar. We suspect that since Abu Nidal never fully trusted any of his operatives, his clones actually perpetrated all these attacks. It has been rumored, moreover, that there are actually two sets of clones: those produced from the moustache hairs resemble Abu Nidal after his plastic surgery while those made from the fingernail clippings resemble him before his plastic surgery.

Carlos Cloned, Too?

The source (who is slowly recovering in an Israeli hospital) had not heard of any other cloning operations, but it seems likely that the infamous international terrorist Ilich Ramirez Sanchez, known as Carlos, was also the beneficiary of this procedure. Absent the existence of cloned duplicates of Carlos, the only logical explanation of why he has been reported in so many parts of the world simultaneously is rampant gullibility in the US Intelligence Community.

Iran: Terrorist Training Program Revealed

A warm and appreciative source close to Iran's Ayatollah Khomeini reports that the key to the Imam's incredible longevity has nothing to do with spiritual fulfillment, genetics, or proper nutrition, or—as has sometimes been alleged—plain and simple meanness. Instead, the key is that the Imam religiously watches and exercises along with the Richard Simmons workout show. Khomeini first started watching the Simmons program when he was in exile in France, and he fervently believes that his daily workouts are what keep his cardiovascular system working well despite the fact that he smokes opium almost continually. Unbeknownst to all but his closest advisors, the Imam actually wears Danskin leotards under his robes all the time so that he is ready to work out whenever he gets the urge.

Khomeini is so enthusiastic about "aerobicize" that he has forced the commander of the Iranian Revolutionary Guard (RG) to use tapes of Simmons's shows to train Iranian-backed terrorist groups. The source said that when Simmons is not taping shows, in fact, the IRG flies him to Iran or the Bekaa Valley to lead the most intense training sessions in person.

The Simmons training program reportedly has other fringe benefits besides producing physically fit terrorists: it is also the reason Iranian-backed terrorists are such willing martyrs. As our source puts it, "After hearing Simmons's voice day in and day out saying 'come on girls, really reach for it' wouldn't you want to kill yourself?"

// ⊕ //

In the Coffee Shop

(Following is a translation of a commercial shown on Syrian State Television (SST) in Damascus several times during the evening of 1 April.)

The camera pans slowly toward two men wearing kafiyas, who are sitting together at a little table, one of several such tables in what is evidently a monumentally grungy coffee shop.

Habbash	"My experience with the PFLP makes me an excellent judge of hand weapons. And my weapon of choice is the Walther P-38. It's a nice handy semiautomatic. But I like it most because it's more lethal than any other hand gun."
Hawatimah	"Well, George. That may be so. But your group hasn't pulled off a major operation in more than five years. We professional terrorists in the DFLP prefer the Walther because it's less visible."
Habbash	"Don't be naïve, Naif. Seriously, you call that shoot-em-up fiasco in Jerusalem last year 'professional'? Your guys ought to learn to use Walthers instead of those silly Kalashnikovs, because they're more lethal."
Hawatimah	"Less visible!"
Habbash	"More lethal!"
Hawatimah	"Less visible!"

As the scuzzy Arab onlookers lunge backward in alarm, Habbash jumps to his feet, pulls out a Walther P-38, hitherto concealed, and empties it into Hawatimah.

Habbash "BLAM-BLAM- BLAM-BLAM- BLAM-BLAM-!"

Hawatimah (gasping) "George, I never dreamed you had a gun. You see, it is less visible! (expires, smiling)

Habbash (scowling at corpse) "More lethal!"
(fadeout)

// ⊕ //

What Is This Thing Called Terrorism?

How many times have we heard the expression, "One man's terrorist is another man's vivisectionist?" This merely points up the deep divisions within the intelligence and policymaking communities regarding the true meaning of the term "terrorism". In this article we propose to pour a little light on troubled waters, to cast a little oil on the subject, as it were.

What Terrorism is Not

The first thing we must do, it seems to us, is to explain what terrorism is not. Terrorism is not nice, for example. We can all agree on that. And terrorism is not polite, either. Beyond these points, consensus has proven difficult to achieve.

Terrorists Versus Insurgents

It is easy to tell insurgents from terrorists. Insurgents operate from bases in territory which they control and govern. If not clean, neatly pressed uniforms, they wear distinctive identifying insignia. They wash often and always have clean fingernails. Their military forces use conventional military tactics to attack legitimate leftwing government military targets and installations. They never hurt civilians or private property or use bad language, and they support the free-enterprise system and are pro-American.

By contrast, terrorists are almost always Communists and anti-American. (In fact, being anti-American is pretty much proof they are Communists.) Terrorists rarely wear uniforms, and when they do the uniforms are not neatly pressed. They often go around dirty. They rant a lot. They attack civilian targets in preference to military ones, and they are very sneaky. They especially target multinational corporations and similar democratic institutions. Sometimes they claim to be insurgents even though they have no base area which they control. This, of course, is not only dishonest but ridiculous.

Terrorist Tactics

The following tactics are deemed to be terrorist tactics when used by subnational groups or covert government agents against Western or other friendly government interests. When they are used by insurgents (see above), they are regrettable momentary lapses better not dwelt upon.

- Armed attack
- Kidnaping
- Hostage and Barricade
- Hijacking
- Arson, incendiary bombing
- Explosive bombing

Navigating the Definitional Morass

A book recently published in the Netherlands contains more than 100 pages of material describing competing definitions of terrorism. This is snotsucking stinktoed Europessimistic hair-splitting. There is no need to define terrorism, really. We all know it when we see it, don't we. If a definition is absolutely required, one of the two that follow should suffice:

- Terrorism is illegitimate violence by objectionable persons in pursuit of unacceptable ends.
- Terrorism is a bucket of warm piss. (Some sources erroneously indicate the liquid is warm spit.)

// 🌐 //

Kasey Muhammad's Terrorism Hit Parade

Place	Song/Artist (Place Last Week)	Weeks on Chart
1.	"Driveway to Heaven" *Abu Haydar and the Suicide Commandos (1)*	65
2.	"Feed the People" *RAF and the Hungerstrikers, with special guest star Bobby Sands (9)*	2
3.	"He Ain't a Terrorist, He's My Brother" *The Musawi Family Singers (2)*	66
4.	"Roman Holiday" *The Ladispoli Seven (4)*	12
5.	"A Bombin' Man Cain't Get Nowhere Today" *Abu Ibrahim and the 15 May Dirtballs (-)*	1
6.	"Please Release Me" *The Dawa Party Chorus of Kuwait (5)*	23
7.	"Mines Under Troubled Waters" *Muammar and the Frogmen (3)*	34
8.	"Blinded by the Light" *Sendero Luminoso and the Fireflies (8)*	6
9.	"Light My Fire" *Chukaku-ha and the Nippon Tucker Band (10)*	3
10.	"You Made Me Shoot You (I Didn't Wanna Do It)" *Mehmet Ali Agca and the Prevaricators (-)*	1

Can't Miss Hit Pick:

"When JSOC Goes Marching In"

Norman's Tabbygrackle Choir

Dark Horse Hit Pick:

"This Land Is Your Land, This Land is My Land"

Yasir Arafat and Meir Kahane

Best New Release:

"The Mideast Martyr Blues"

Ayatollah Rockanrollah with Shaykh Djibouti

// 🌐 //

"The Mideast Martyr Blues"

© Fast Food for Thought Records, 1 April 1985

Tune: "Two all-beef patties..."
Two automatic Uzis,
Special SAMs,
RPGs,
And a Scorpion
Make a cache of great guns

Tune: "Slow down Roy Rogers says..."
Mow 'em down,
Khomeini says, more.
This might be bloody stuff, a bit too much gore,
But it's the kind you die for.

Tune: "Kentucky Fried Chicken..."
Islamic Jihad:
They do it right.
Islamic Jihad:
They do terror right.

// 🌐 //

Was It Something I Said?

Following are the lyrics of a song recently published in an Iranian magazine. Although the words do not rhyme and the meter is irregular, the sincerely of the lyricist shines through.

Tune: "Let Me Call You Sweetheart"
America, America, shame on you, the foul fiend.
From your evil claws, the blood of our youngsters drips.
The ferocious flames of your fetid deeds,

Aflame have set the entire world.
The global safety and security,
Upset have been by your fraudulent tricks
Every corner of the world, far and nigh,
Bears the cruel tint of your cantankerous crimes.
Your hoarded riches, superfluous as they are,
Upon the pains of the world deprived have been built.
The daggers of your hatred deep,
Many a brave breast apart have torn.
A world-devouring pilferer of low descent,
A truculent, savage ghoul you are.
A lethal, venomous-natured scorpion,
A cool-hearted, cunning fox you are.
Replete with treachery, pure perfidy,
Deplete of compassion and love you are.
Of devilry and dread your being reeks,
Vainly void of the elixir of good you are.
Through the entire history of man,
Surpassed you have all in desperate diablerie.
Entangled in every net of conspiracy you are.
No token of love in your hate-laden heart.
America, America, shame on you, the foul fiend.
In every corner of the whole wide world,
Your fickle flames of frenzy fly.
Nauseated to death, the whole wide world,
Weeps in agony by your so-called "Human Rights"
An index of satanic brutality indeed,
An indelible stain of shame you are,
A devil incarnate, a crime-ridden imp,
Rebellion seethes in your polluted blood.
In mind, you only nurture the notion how
To lay waste the globe entire.
Befogged, benighted by your ruses dark,
The whole wide world does mourn and cry.
You, the enemy of every nation

You, the cause of every abjection
You, the shade of every shame
You, the disrupter of every heart.

//🌐//

Chronology of Terrorism—1 April 1985

Luxembourg: Mysterious, swarthy Middle Eastern types arrested at international airport. Muhammad Ali Husayn, Ali Husayn Muhammad, and Husayn Ali Muhammad, all traveling on South Yemeni diplomatic passports, are being held without bond pending completion of name traces. They claimed to be en route to Baden Baden to attend an international hairdressers convention. They had no idea how the 300 kilograms of Semtex-H came to be in their luggage.

Portugal: FP-25 terrorists miss again. Ten operatives of the Popular Forces of 25 April (FP-25) brandishing chrome-plated pistols surrounded recreational-vehicle magnate Deke Pereira at close range and opened fire on him, continuing to fire until he became bored and summoned police. Four of the terrorists were killed outright by the internecine gunfire, and another was captured after he tripped and broke his leg while running away. The remaining five escaped, but police are not concerned. "They couldn't hit a barn from inside it," one said.

Portugal: FP-25 mortar recovered from Lisbon harbor. Tests indicate the weapon, found in shallow water near a fishing pier, was the same one used to attack the US Embassy and various NATO installations in the Lisbon area in recent months. Close examination revealed the tube was curved like a huge piece of elbow macaroni. "No wonder they never hit anybody with it," a US Embassy spokesman commented, after the weapon had been presented to the Embassy for conversion into an umbrella stand.

United States: Libyan ship sinks under mysterious circumstances in Baltimore harbor. Investigations subsequently revealed the SS "Muammar Sunshine" had hit a mine left over from the US Civil War. The ship had been carrying a load of counterfeit Cabbage Patch dolls from North

Korea. The Cuban captain and the Nicaraguan crew were rescued by the Coast Guard cutter "Baltimore Oreo".

United States: Beverly Hills home of aerobics guru Richard Simmons destroyed by suicide car bomber. Witnesses said a swarthy, Arab-looking male drove a Winnebago evidently loaded with explosives right into Simmons's workout room. As he careened up the driveway, the driver reportedly screamed in broken English, "I can't take it anymore!" An anonymous caller to a local newspaper claimed the Islamic Jihad was responsible.

United States: Lebanese terrorist safehouse raided in Watts. Police seized a small arsenal of weapons, 10 kilograms of plastic explosive, several posters of the Ayatollah Khomeini, and detailed drawings of the Beverly Hills mansion of Richard Simmons. The safehouse was discovered after neighbors complained of continuous, loud whining music and shouts of Ash 'alha! (Arabic for "Make it burn!") In a VCR in the safehouse was found a Taiwan-made counterfeit copy of the newest version of the Jane Fonda workout tape.

West Germany: RAF terrorists sinking badly. Three members of the hardcore "guerrilla" of the Red Army Faction disappeared today while attempting to service a weapons cache concealed in a quicksand pit near Offenbach. They are presumed dead. Expression of condolence and contributions to the cause may be sent to Rote Hilfe, in care of this publication.

West Germany: RAF terrorist gets it in gear. Red Army Faction operative Manfred Stolid was arrested today without a struggle in a suburb of Gerolsteinerspruedelwasserhafn, after his stolen car rolled backwards and pinned him to a telephone pole while he was trying to attach a forged "doublet" license plate.

Iran: Ayatollah Khomeini escaped assassination attempt. As he was completing the 21st mile of the inaugural Qum Muslim Marathon, Khomeini was shot at by several assailants. Since they missed, they were probably Iranians, or maybe Arabs, you know how bad they shoot.

Iraq: Fertilizer plant outside Baghdad explodes, exuding massive cloud of gas. A subsequent radio broadcast by Saddam Hussein denying Iranian claims of sabotage and reassuring the Iraqi people was cut short when the President burst into a coughing fit. Since then, Iraq has maintained total radio silence.

Jordan: King Hussein and Yasir Arafat form travel agency. "They're just tired of the same old camel race," said Queen Noor. They are to be joined by Abu Nidal, once he finishes making a movie in Japan. The agency will specialize in arranging trips to the sites of famous terrorist incidents, according to a Royal press release.

Lebanon: Walt Disney firm plans extravagant amusement complex in Bekaa Valley. To be called "Militiaworld", the complex will feature "the various feisty factions of the Lebanese in their distinctive native costumes and hardware," according to a Disney press release. Supervising the construction of the project will be Mr. Al Banna, a local entrepreneur.

Libya: Briefcase plant disappears in huge fireball. Early suspicions that the blast was the result of terrorism seem not to have been borne out. "It was probably just some chemical thingee," a government spokesman explained.

Syria: PFLP holds reunion in Damascus. Present at the festivities hosted by jovial PFLP patriarch George Habbash were members of his own organization, plus representatives of the PFLP-General Command, the PFLP-Special Command, the 15 May Organization (representing the defunct PFLP-Special Operations Group and its predecessor, the PFLP Special Operations Committee), the DFLP, and the PDFLP. All present really enjoyed themselves chatting about past exploits. Then they all piled into a truck, drove to the Israeli border, and lobbed a few rounds into a schoolhouse for old times' sake.

Ecuador: New rightwing terrorist group stampedes livestock; hundreds trampled to death. In Quito, a mysterious new rightwing terrorist group calling itself "Alfaro Morte, Carajo!" (Alfaro is dead, damnit!) announced its formation by donating a small propaganda bomb at a cattle auction.

Peru: Terrorist group disbands in despair. Members of the leftwing urban guerrilla group Sendero Doloroso (Gloomy Path) decided to cease operations after concluding that life is meaningless.

Zaire: New terrorist groups discovered. A search of the office of the Minister of the Interior revealed he had emigrated seven weeks earlier, having lost control of his files. They proved to contain evidence of the following previously unknown terrorist and insurgent groups in Zaire: ZPLP, MLZ, PLFZ, ZROG, DZROG, BLOATZ, BLOATZ-M/L, BLOATZ-M/L-Urban Faction, and the Kinshasa Joyous Flux. No further information could be gleaned from the rotting, crumbling papers found blowing around the Minister's office.

Sri Lanka: Last Sinhalese killed in Colombo. Tamil separatist guerrillas ultimately failed to provoke the Sinhalese backlash they had so long been seeking, when they shot to death the last ethnic Sinhalese left alive on the island, Colombo grocer George Guffawandslapaknee. Just before he died, the victim was heard to say, "I simply refuse to become provoked."

GLOSSARY

No self-disrespecting guide to intelligence humor would be complete without a guide to some of the acronyms involved. (This book's sections on military issues include numerous Pentagonese acronyms. We're just going to walk away, slowly, from these.) In addition to the ones we met in the first volume of this series, let us consider:

// 🌐 //

BOGSAT literally, Bunch of Guys Sitting Around a Table, despite every effort to introduce rigor to intelligence analysis, remains the most commonly conducted collaboration method in the IC

// 🌐 //

CTU: Counter Terrorism Unit, or Counter Terrorist Unit, depending upon the season of 24 you're watching. Alas, CTU doesn't really exist. Jack Bauer does. And so does Nina, although she now seems to be Annie's boss in Covert Affairs.

// 🌐 //

Retired on Active Duty, a Navy term for somebody who stopped working years ago but still shows up to collect a paycheck

// 🌐 //

Rumor Intelligence (RUMINT), an information intelligence source often with indirect or imagined access to information. Often used as slang for gossip, scuttlebutt, or other information learned through non-official channels. RUMINT typically covers information such as personnel changes, pay issues, early release for holidays (which still remains the most quickly-disseminated intelligence in any IC agency), and other issues typically considered immutable by general employees and non-critical to actual work.

Subcategories of RUMINT include Myth Intelligence (MYTHINT) and Bogus Intelligence (BOGINT). RUMINT that proves to be false is sometimes categorized as ISINT.

RUMINT is sometimes used by maritime personnel to refer to locations of good bars (literally, rum intelligence), likely in reference to rum's historical ties to sea trade.

// 🌐 //

Myth Intelligence (also Mythical Intelligence) (MYTHINT) refers to intelligence activities or institutional knowledge of such activities within the IC concerning events, technology, or individuals assumed to be connected to past and current intelligence operations, although in all likelihood are highly improbable if not outright impossible.

Given the nebulous nature of intelligence work and "need to know" standards, MYTHINT inherently takes on a legendary quality, seemingly historic yet with no way to fully prove or disprove claims. Bogus Intelligence (BOGINT) differs from MYTHINT in that BOGINT can and is often disproved. MYTHINT typically fades or resurfaces due to major personnel changes where institutional knowledge s lost or regained due to retirements, reassignments, or larger reorganizations.

A myth example: There is a thick layer of magnesium that spans the roofing of every major intelligence agency. In the event of a massive breach of national security i.e., foreign military invasion, successful coup d'etat, etc.), an anonymous trusted agent within the agency is authorized to ignite he magnesium, thus instantly incinerating the building, melting its contents and driving the entire amalgam deep underground. In reality, this only exists at NSA (or name-of-your-organization here, depending upon where you work).

// 🌐 //

Some words sound and look the same, but mean entirely different things to different organizations. For example, "secure the building".

- Marines get inside the building, then point their guns outward.
- The Army points their guns at the building.
- The Navy changes the locks on the building.
- The Air Force obtains a 5-year lease for the building and sends in cleaning crews.

www.ingramcontent.com/pod-product-compliance
Lightning Source LLC
Chambersburg PA
CBHW070106120526
44588CB00032B/1183
* 9 7 8 1 9 4 9 1 7 3 0 1 7 *